CHICAGO PUBLIC LIBRARY

0 S. STATE ST.   60605

CIAL SCIENCES & HISTORY DIVISION

CHICAGO PUBLIC LIBRARY

R01050 28313

D1564434

CHICAGO PUBLIC LIBRARY

400 S. STATE ST.   60605

SOCIAL SCIENCES & HISTORY DIVISION

Agricultural Ethics:
Issues for the 21st Century

CHICAGO PUBLIC LIBRARY

400 S. STATE ST.   6065

Agricultural Ethics: Issues for the 21st Century

Proceedings of a symposium sponsored by the Soil Science Society of America, American Society of Agronomy, and the Crop Science Society of America in Minneapolis, MN, Oct. 31–Nov. 5 1992. Organized by Division S-3 (Soil Biology and Biochemistry).

Organizing Committee
Peter G. Hartel
Horace D. Skipper
Thomas A Ruehr

Editorial Committee
Peter G. Hartel
Kathryn Paxton George
James Vorst

Managing Editor
David M. Kral

Associate Editor
Pamm Kasper

ASA Special Publication Number 57

Soil Science Society of America, Inc.
American Society of Agronomy, Inc.
Crop Science Society of America, Inc.
Madison, Wisconsin, USA

1994

Cover design: "Typhwheate" (*Triticum durum* Desf.) adapted from an illustration in *Nievve Herball* by Rembet Dodoens, translated by Henry Lyte in 1578. "Typhwheate," or pasta wheat, is one of the Old World races of wheat. Wheat exhibits a beauty of form and function that is characteristic of nature; consciousness of such a value is one basis of agricultural ethics.

Copyright © 1994 by the Soil Science Society of America, Inc.
American Society of Agronomy, Inc.
Crop Science Society of America, Inc.

ALL RIGHTS RESERVED UNDER THE U.S. COPYRIGHT LAW OF 1978 (P.L. 94-553)

Any and all uses beyond the limitations of the "fair use" provision of the law require written permission from the publisher(s) and/or the author(s); not applicable to contributions prepared by officers or employees of the U.S. Government as part of their official duties.

Soil Science Society of America, Inc.
American Society of Agronomy, Inc.
Crop Science Society of America, Inc.
677 South Segoe Road
Madison, WI 53711

Library of Congress Cataloging-in-Publication Data

Agricultural ethics: issues for the 21st century: proceedings of a symposium sponsored by the Soil Science Society of America, American Society of Agronomy, and the Crop Science Society of America in Minneapolis, MN, Oct. 31–Nov. 5, 1992 / organized by Division S-3 (Soil Biology and Biochemistry); organizing committee, Peter G. Hartel, Horace D. Skipper, Thomas A. Ruehr; editorial committee, Peter G. Hartel, Kathryn Paxton George, James Vorst.

     p.   cm. — (ASA special publication; no. 57)
    Includes bibliographical references.
    ISBN 0-89118-121-0
    1. Agriculture—Moral and ethical aspects—Congresses.
I. Hartel, Peter. II. George, Kathryn Paxton. III. Vorst, James. IV. Soil Science Society of America. V. American Society of Agronomy. VI. Crop Science Society of America. VII. Soil Science Society of America. Division S-3. VIII. Series.
BJ52.5.A37 1994   94-25924
174'.963—dc20   CIP

CHICAGO PUBLIC LIBRARY

RO1050 28313

400 S. STATE ST.   60605

SOCIAL SCIENCES & HISTORY DIVISION

CONTENTS

CHICAGO PUBLIC LIBRARY

400 S. STATE ST.   60605

FOREWORD

Practitioners of agriculture have ethical or acceptable behavioral traits as do the more widely recognized professions such as medicine or law. This is not new — we have long recognized the "land ethic" of farmers, who value the care of their land as security for future generations. Ethics, or the lack of them, have been thrust upon us in agriculture dramatically in the past few years. Agricultural ethics have many forms, but as the authors of this book point out, a holistic view and concept of ethics is essential for the well-being of people and the environment in which they live. When the principles of agricultural ethics are fully articulated, they can then be taught and practiced. The framework will be set for judgment of acceptable behavior of agriculturalists as stewards of soil, water, and biological resources and as providers of safe and nutritious food and fibers. This is urgently needed as evidenced by the questioning of current practices in agricultural production with respect to the use of pesticides and fertilizers, soil degradation, and the eminent introduction of products of biotechnology that call on genes from totally unrelated organisms to improve our crops and livestock. As the editors point out, this small book could not address all of the issues nor could it provide comprehensive depth of inquiry in all aspects of agricultural ethics, but it is a critical introduction and we hope that educators will use this book as an introduction to the complexity and importance of the subject. The organizers of the symposium and authors are to be commended for this effort. We encourage the members of the Tri-Societies to engage this emerging field and to contribute to its development.

Calvin O. Qualset
President
American Society of
Agronomy

Vernon B. Cardwell
President
Crop Science Society
of America

Larry P. Wilding
President
Soil Science Society of
America

PREFACE

When teachers of agricultural ethics were first told about this symposium, almost all of them replied, "It's about time." We understood why they said this. The collective membership of the Tri-Societies has had very little to say or write on agricultural ethics. *Agriculture and Human Values*, one of the premier journals in the field, has published 304 authors from its inception in 1984 to 1992, yet only two (<1%!) listed any affiliation with agronomy, crop science, or soil science. That is why "it's about time." As this was the first Tri-Societies symposium ever held, we think it fitting that the subject be agricultural ethics.

What is agricultural ethics and why do we need to talk about it? Agricultural ethics looks at the philosophical, social, political, legal, economic, scientific, and aesthetic aspects of agricultural problems and provides guidance for decisions about these problems when they involve competing values. We realize that many of our students do not know how to make decisions involving competing values, and this is one of the reasons that agricultural ethics became one of the highest priority needs in agricultural curricula (Merritt, 1984). If our goal is to provide an adequate, healthy, and sustainable supply of food and fiber by means that respect the rights and dignity of all participants in the food production system, then an integration of ethics and agriculture should form the basis of decisions that are sensitive to technology and capable of protecting the common good (Dundon, 1987).

Agricultural ethics is a holistic way of thinking — a point that several authors in this book reinforce. If we are conducting research in agricultural biotechnology, then agricultural ethics makes us consider automatically the socioeconomic costs of this research. For those of us who are research scientists and have based our entire lives on scientific reductionism (thinking about science in its smallest increment to say what is true or not true), this is not easy. Some scientists have begun to look holistically at agricultural research and do not like what they see. They cannot justify supporting agriculture as a powerful technology that seems to put small farmers out of business, displaces indigenous people, degrades the environment, and causes unpredictable economic effects (Crouch, 1990). The resulting tension drives them out of science. Others search for alternatives that combine their research with increased ethical training (Medford and Flores, 1990). This is a major point in agricultural ethics: social responsibility goes hand in hand with scientific responsibility (Smith, 1990).

To integrate one's considered ethical values into decisions and actions is difficult. Most of us have never had a formal course in ethics. The two authors in this publication who are members of the Tri-Societies, Peter G. Hartel and Thomas A Ruehr, have exactly one three-credit-hour course in philosophy between them. For this reason, this book contains a chapter on ethical theory by Frederick Ferré, a distinguished professor of philosophy. We have tried to minimize the philosophical jargon throughout the book and have included a glossary of philosophical terms as an additional aid.

Our readers may ask why all except two of the authors in this publication are from outside the Tri-Societies. To quote the poet, Robert Burns, "O wad some Pow'r the giftie gie us, To see oursels as others see us!" ("To a louse"; Kingsley, 1969). These "outside" authors know the practical side of the problems that we face: all have written before on agricultural ethics; some have been connected with agriculture for many years; some have grown up on farms. Some were selected because we knew that they would tell us things that we did not want to hear. While all the authors were asked to give a balanced presentation, they were asked also to "speak their own minds." Several have done this.

It is not possible to cover the entire spectrum of agricultural ethics in a four-hour symposium. There are many topics that were not addressed. For instance, at the end of the symposium, a vigorous discussion ensued about the role of university scientists conducting patentable research. Should public universities, which are ultimately supported by taxpayers, support private research? It rapidly became clear that many did not share the same views. It is important to note that each chapter in this book represents the vision of only one person. We regard many of these chapters simply as starting points for discussion. As teachers of agricultural ethics, we can vouch that the topics covered in this book (animal welfare and animal rights, conventional vs. alternative agriculture, and world hunger) can (and do!) occupy literally weeks of classroom discussion.

We would like to thank Mona Freer for her editing, and Gail Jones and Teresa Facer for their assistance in manuscript preparation. Finally, we thank the leadership of the Tri-Societies for allowing us (through member dues) to bring the outside speakers to the annual meeting.

Peter G. Hartel   Kathryn Paxton George   James Vorst
University of Georgia   *University of Idaho*   *Purdue University*
Athens, Georgia   *Moscow, Idaho*   *West Lafayette, Indiana*

References

Crouch, M.L. 1990. Debating the responsibilities of plant scientists in the decade of the environment. Plant Cell 2:275–277.

Dundon, S J. 1987. On the cultivation of morals. Calif. Farmer 32:5–6.

Kingsley, J. 1969. Burns' poems and songs. Oxford Univ. Press, London.

Medford, J I., and H.E. Flores. 1990. Plant scientists' responsibilities: An alternative. Plant Cell 2:501–502.

Merritt, R.H. 1984. Challenges for undergraduate education in agricultural sciences. NACTA J. 28:9–14.

Smith, S.E. 1990. Plant biology and social responsibility. Plant Cell 2:367–368.

1   Overview

Peter G. Hartel

University of Georgia
Athens, Georgia

Thinking about Agricultural Ethics

Agricultural ethics contains one of those "uh-oh" words; while we have a
pretty good idea of what *agriculture* is, *ethics* may be a different matter. It
reminds me of when my son was three years old and asked, "Dad, what do
you do?" I said (not without a little pride in my voice), "Ben, I'm a
microbiologist." Then I thought of how many syllables were in those words
and how old my son was, so I asked, "Can you say that?" And he replied,
"Macaroni." My point is that unless you've had a course in philosophy, you
may not have a very good idea of what ethics is. Well, ethics is nothing more
than the basis of why something is good or bad or right or wrong.

Whether or not you consider something good or bad or right or wrong
depends on your values. These values, which combine to give each of us a set
of moral principles, are the foundation of ethics. When we think about ethical
problems in agriculture, we would like to make our decisions in a rational,
emotionally cool manner that clearly defines the problem, considers all the
information at hand, *and* is in keeping with our values. We may still have a
problem though: the word *values* makes us uncomfortable. To see why this is
so, let's look at values the way the Greeks did. For the Greeks, something
could be valued two ways: something could have *instrumental* value, which
is its usefulness to humans, or something could have *intrinsic* value, which is
value for its own sake, independent of its usefulness. The source of our
discomfort is that while we are good at thinking about instrumental value
(what is something's usefulness to us?), we are not so good at thinking about
intrinsic value. Why is this? It is because we think of intrinsic value as a
subjective, irrational expression of emotion. For those of us in agriculture, this
is the hardest part of thinking ethically: that a value can have value precisely
because it cannot be priced.

We need to spend more time thinking about intrinsic value. One reason
to do this is that we then begin to think more holistically. That is why
agricultural ethics can include aesthetics, which we may not have considered

Copyright © 1994 American Society of Agronomy, Crop Science Society of America, Soil Science
Society of America, 677 S. Segoe Rd., Madison, WI 53711, USA. *Agricultural Ethics: Issues for
the 21st Century*, ASA Special Publication no. 57.

before in our decision-making. On the cover of this publication is a picture of wheat. Wheat exhibits a beauty of form and function that is characteristic of nature, and consciousness of such a value is one basis of agricultural ethics. For many of us, wheat *is* beautiful; therefore, agricultural ethics makes us think across a broader spectrum. In his chapter, "Teaching Agricultural Ethics," Thomas A Ruehr speaks of the difficulty of getting scientists to move beyond their narrow specialities and to become more interdisciplinary. Ethical problems are interdisciplinary and require a holistic (or systemic) approach. Holistic thinking will serve us much better in resolving the agricultural problems of the 21st century than the scientific reductionism that is so prevalent today.

Another reason to think about intrinsic value is that it forces us to confront what some philosophers (e.g., Shrader-Fréchette, 1994) refer to as the "dangerous myth": that somehow neutrality equals objectivity. We are often afraid to speak up because we think that we will not appear to be objective. The problem with this myth is that when we don't say anything, we may simply end up reinforcing the status quo. We need to be more inclined to challenge the status quo because when there are reasons to favor one position over another, we come closer to the truth by taking a position on the issue, not by remaining neutral (Davion, 1994). This dangerous myth can keep us from saying what we think when what we think may be extremely important.

From the myriad issues that agricultural ethics covers, this publication focuses on three major ones: animal rights and animal welfare, conventional vs. alternative agriculture, and world hunger. They were selected because more people today think we are going in the wrong direction on these issues than any other. Many are uncomfortable with an agricultural system whose economic policies ignore future generations and discount environmental degradation, whose policies do little to support rural communities, and whose aid programs — despite their good intentions — weaken indigenous agriculture elsewhere. Many fear that feeding more than 10 billion people in 2050 will not be possible. These are some of the really important problems in agricultural ethics, and we need to talk about them.

Animal Rights and Animal Welfare

Today, there are some 400 animal protection groups in the USA, with a combined membership of 10 million and a total budget of $50 million (Kaufmann, 1993). Their memberships continue to grow rapidly, meaning that animal rights and animal welfare concerns have the potential to become a great challenge for U.S. agriculture in the next century.

To understand animal rights and animal welfare, it is important to know that each group represents one of two major conceptual paths in ethics. One path is based on consequences, the other on rights and duties. Animal welfarists want to eliminate practices that result in stress, pain, and suffering in animals. Because every practice has degrees of good and bad, the animal welfarist would like to maximize the good and find the practice with the best net welfare. Because each practice has a consequence, animal welfarists' arguments are consequentialist or teleological (from the Greek *telos*, end or purpose). In his chapter, "No Hiding Place: The Inescapability of Agricultural Ethics," Frederick Ferré simplifies these philosophical terms even further as *aim ethics* — only the outcome of an action (its consequences) counts. An example is utilitarianism, which is a comparison of benefits and harms such that the greatest good for the greatest number is the best course.

In contrast, animal rights are not based on consequences but on rights and duties. An animal rightist not only considers animals worthy of moral consideration, but also enlarges this consideration to such an extent as to consider it plausible that animals may act in pursuit of their own chosen interests. If animals can do this, then they are worthy of moral rights. Alternatively, if the properties by which humans are said to possess certain rights that are not uniquely human (e.g., sentience, ability to communicate, ability to suffer), then there is no reason to restrict the possession of rights uniquely to humans. Since these are not consequences, animal rights arguments are nonconsequentialist or deontological (from the Greek *deont*, duty or obligation). Ferré simplifies nonconsequentialist theory to *rule ethics* since only the principle (one's obligations) counts.

While our views on animals represent a spectrum, it is important to understand that consequentialist arguments cannot be used against nonconsequentialist arguments and vice versa. For example, as an institution, democracy is consequentialist because it represents what the majority wants; however, the Bill of Rights in the U.S. Constitution is nonconsequentialist because it bestows certain rights. You cannot use democracy against the Bill of Rights; I have a right to free speech and it does not matter what you or the majority wants. For an animal rightist, there is no scientific justification for something that is morally wrong (Zak, 1989). Although the majority of the membership of the Tri-Societies is undoubtedly strongly animal welfarist (because most scientists are utilitarians), we are going to have trouble talking with animal rightists because we cannot use scientific justification — a teleological argument — against a principle — a deontological argument. We can only talk to animal rightists on a deontological basis: are animals morally considerable beings? How do humans and animals differ and are these differences morally relevant?

It is also important to understand that consequentalist thinking can yield only one "right" answer. For the animal welfarist, there is only *one* practice that will result in the best net welfare. Alternatively, as long as a certain threshold is exceeded, nonconsequentalist thinking allows many "right" answers. For an animal rightist, defining the threshold is what is important. If the threshold is sentience, then an animal rightist might never condone the killing of a pig, a relatively intelligent animal, but might think nothing of eating a clam. It is incorrect for animal welfarists to assume that the only view held by animal rightists is the complete dissolution of commercial animal agriculture. This represents only the extreme view. The members of the Tri-Societies who are animal welfarists must remember the differences between consequentalist and nonconsequentalist thinking. These are apples and oranges. Because rights are not empirical — they are conceptual and involve intrinsic value — I do not underestimate how difficult this is. But if animal welfarists and animal rightists are to communicate with each other, then this is where communication begins.

In the 21st century, there will be two potential sources of conflict for agriculture and animal welfarists. The first is humaneness (Fig. 1). Veal production is considered the most inhumane practice in agriculture, and this practice will be singled out by some animal welfarists for elimination. It is considered inhumane because some veal calves are kept in a restricted space and fed only milk. This practice produces a meat that is tender and light-colored, but the restricted space deprives the calf of normal movement, and the iron-deficient diet leads to anemia. In the case of anemia, many people cannot justify incurring a pathological condition in an animal in order to eat its meat. These practices are the reason you see advertisements against veal production in various periodicals. To its credit, the veal industry has responded to these criticisms by trying to eliminate milk-fed veal and to educate consumers that veal doesn't have to be pale pink in color (calves fed an adequate amount of iron will have a meat that is redder but equally tender). Similarly, more veal calves are being kept in open stalls that allow freedom of movement and social interaction. I think the 21st century will see agriculturists as more humane, more conscientious, and more accountable than we are now.

Product	Humaneness	Example of typical condition
Veal	less	milk-fed veal kept in small crates
Eggs		layer hens kept in battery cages
Pork, ham, bacon		breeding sows often confined in stalls
		or tethered on a short chain
Lamb, mutton		indiscrimate predator control
		(Western United States)
Beef		overgrazing of rangeland
Turkey, duck, chicken		factory farming
Milk, butter, cheese	more	factory farming

Fig. 1. Humaneness of some animal husbandry practices for the production of some animal products (adapted from Fox, 1983).

The other source of conflict for agriculture and animal welfare organizations will be technology, particularly as it relates to intensive animal production. Often referred to as "factory farming", intensive animal production requires that a large number of animals be confined to a restricted space for extended periods of time. Consider dairy farming, which most of us would agree is a relatively humane animal husbandry practice. In the past, increased milk production was directly linked to increased animal welfare (Albright, 1983). In fact, maximum efficiency of milk production depended on a close human bond. We now have, however, the technological means to increase milk production at the expense of animal welfare. In the case of intensive animal production, the reasons for criticism are an increased dependence on mechanization (if things go wrong, they can go wrong in a big way), a decreased psychological well-being (where each cow receives less individual attention), and an increased production stress (where energy-dense rations lead to increased digestive disorders and a shortened life span) (Thompson et al., 1994). In his chapter, "Farm Animal Welfare: Obligations, Realities, and Compromises," Stanley E. Curtis emphasizes a "minimal ethically acceptable condition," where we have an obligation to make sure our technology is appropriate. For example, if we are to stimulate milk production in dairy cows with bovine somatropin, we need to be sure that this is not at the expense of the cows' welfare.

Even though recommendations and regulations on the treatment of animals have generally been resisted by the agricultural industry (Albright, 1983), there is much common ground between agriculture and animal rights and animal welfare organizations. Everyone agrees that there is no long-term economic justification for animal sickness and suffering and that we need to increase our communication. It is up to us to remember that we will have continued uncertainty and conflict because we have neither perfect knowledge nor a perfect agreement of values.

Alternative vs. Conventional Agriculture

Arguments between alternative and conventional agriculture have been going on since the beginning of agriculture. Perhaps the easiest way to see this conflict is to ask a simple question: Is agriculture a business? If you agree that agriculture is a business, then there tends to be a cascade of things with which you will also agree. These are competitiveness, with an emphasis on speed, quantity, and profit; centralization, with a concentrated control of land, resources, and capital; and specialization, with a heavy use of science and technology (Beus et al., 1991). Alternatively, you may regard agriculture not as a business but as a way of life. In this instance, the cascade of things with which you will also tend to agree are community, with an emphasis on permanence, quality, and beauty; decentralization, with dispersed control of land, resources, and capital; and nonspecialization, with an emphasis on personal knowledge and local wisdom (Beus et al., 1991). Not surprisingly, most religions, with their strong social agendas, strongly support agriculture as a way of life (Dundon, 1991).

It is easy to see the sources of conflict. Consider centralization. The number of farms in the USA is decreasing and farm size is increasing. In 1981, 298 000 U.S. farms with sales of $100 000 or more accounted for two-thirds of all farm output (Tweeten, 1991). If current trends continue, by the year 2000, only 50 000 large farms will account for two-thirds of all farm output. The message here is "get big or get out." Do we want more large farms?

Consider monocultures. Monocultures are good because they are easy to plant, easy to harvest, and produce a uniform product. Above all, they result in large quantities of products, which results in low prices that consumers want. This is favored by agriculture as a business. Nevertheless, monocultures do not support genetic diversity. Of the thousands of plant species that are edible and adequate for human consumption, only 20 now produce the vast majority of food for the world (Swanson, 1991). When large hectarage is placed into a single crop and a disease or insect becomes adapted to that crop, there is the potential for an epidemic spread of that disease or insect (Duvick, 1991). Are monocultures such a good idea?

Consider energy. Agriculture as a business in the USA is based on the intensive use of petrochemicals. Estimates vary, but generally 5 to 12 calories of fossil fuel energy are required to produce one calorie of food (Berry, 1977). Yet draft animal farming (because one can take advantage of the "free" energy that nature provides in terms of pastures, and one also can recycle manures) yields 30 to 300 food calories for every energy calorie (Cox and Atkins, 1979). Do we really want to return to an earlier age of draft animal farming?

Consider specialization. Land grant institutions, through their support of technology, support agriculture as a business. As Gary Comstock points out in his chapter, "Some Virtues and Vices of Agricultural Biotechnology," land grant institutions have been criticized because they do not consider the socioeconomic impact of their research (e.g., Hightower, 1973). Perhaps we should consider a more "appropriate" technology, one that does not replace or disrupt anything good that already exists, including family and community relationships (Berry, 1990). For those of us in academia, technology driven by specialization also underscores another important ethical point: research is not value free (Madden, 1991). Should land grant institutions be making a bigger effort to support agriculture as a way of life?

The engine that drives agriculture as a business is profit. This is good. A farmer who does not make a profit is soon out of business. However, some things have been left out of the economic equation — what economists (e.g., Madden, 1991) call *externalities*. Among these externalities is environmental degradation. Take soil erosion. Because soil losses are subtle and we live such a short time, we need a long-term example. In 1791, William Bartram, a botanist, wrote a book on his travels throughout the southeastern USA

(Bartram, 1791). One of the places he traveled was Clarke County, Georgia, which is where I live. Bartram described the soil as "a deep, rich, dark mould, on a deep stratum of reddish brown tenacious clay." Today, the soil survey of Clarke County reads "... in much of this acreage [sic], so much material has been lost through erosion that the plow layer now extends into the subsoil" (Soil Conservation Service, 1968). This is the legacy of 100 years of cotton farming: the top 20 cm of the A horizon over a wide hectarage in Clarke County is gone. A mere 10 km from my doorstep, in neighboring Oconee County, farmers in the 1940s growing continuous cotton on a 7% slope might typically lose 25 tons of soil per acre [sic] per year (Carreker and Barnett, 1949). (It is interesting to think that the expression of "red Georgia clay" might not have existed around here without this topsoil loss since the topsoil was clearly a rich dark brown!) This soil loss is unacceptable, but as an externality, it is not considered an economic loss. Who cares if our soil slips seaward?

In the coming century, I think the major conflict between conventional vs. alternative agriculture will be on the concern for environmental degradation. As with agriculture and animal welfare, there is common ground. Everyone agrees that we farm to farm again (Wojcik, 1989). Since heavy soil losses are not sustainable, we can expect conventional agriculture to put environmental degradation back into its economic equation. This is precisely one point of the chapter by Charles V. Blatz, "Coming Full Circle: Ethical Issues in Traditional and Industrialized Agriculture." In the next century, we should expect to see some movement on the part of conventional (industrialized) agriculture to adopt some of the practices of alternative (traditional) agriculture. This is already occurring, as exhibited by a plethora of new scientific journals in this area. It is imperative that we talk about this change because, as my next topic suggests, we also need to have *intergenerational equity*, the ability to provide for today without compromising the ability to provide for future generations (World Commission on Environment and Development, 1987).

World Hunger

This year an estimated 10 million people will starve to death. These people will not die because of an inadequate supply of food, but rather from the lack of money to buy food or as a result of political and social upheaval. However, our continued population growth and our depletion of "renewable" resources suggest that maintaining an adequate supply of food will be a tremendous challenge for agriculture in our future.

The most likely projection of human population growth predicts a near doubling of world population to 10 billion by 2050 (United Nations Population Fund [UNPFA], 1992). Although worldwide fertility rates are declining, the world population continues to grow at record rates. In 1991, the world population grew by a record 92 million people. This was not unusual; a new record has been set every year since 1975, and ahead of us lie four decades of the fastest growth in human numbers in all history (UNPFA, 1992). Almost all of this population growth will be in Africa, Asia, and Latin America. For example, the population of Nigeria, already Africa's most populous nation, will increase from 109 million in 1990 to 281 million by 2025. This is a 258% increase. In contrast, the U.S. population is expected to increase only from 249 million in 1990 to 300 million by 2025, a 26% increase. What is troubling about all of this is that world food output is slowing: for example, grain production per person fell 6% from 1984 to 1992 (Brown, 1993). Many countries in Africa have had high population rates with declining per capita grain consumption for even longer periods of time (Table 1). If real food shortages occur, who will feed these people?

Along with this population growth and loss of food production is the trend of "renewable" resources becoming nonrenewable. The total additional land required to meet the needs of population growth between now and 2050 will be 4.5 million km^2, an increase of 56% of the arable area of developing countries (UNPFA, 1992). Since the limits of suitable land have already been approached or exceeded in many areas of the world, this will require either increased yields or use of less suitable land. Unfortunately, increased yields can only be achieved by the increasing use of chemical fertilizers, a costly practice that is not sustainable over the long term. Likewise, use of marginal land for agriculture may result in increased environmental degradation. As C. Dean Freudenberger points out in his chapter, "What is Good Agriculture?," desertification, salinization, and urbanization of rural land are already commonplace in many developing countries. Furthermore, today 26 countries, collectively home to 232 million people, are now considered water scarce, such that lack of water is a severe constraint on food production (Postel, 1993). By

Table 1. Selected African countries with rapid population growth (adapted from United Nations Population Fund, 1992) and declining per capita grain production, 1970–1985 (adapted from U.S. Department of Agriculture, 1986).

Country	Average growth rate, 1990–1995	Grain production	
		Annual change	Total change
		------------%------------	
Zambia	3.8	−2.2	−25.0
Uganda	3.7	−1.6	−19.0
Kenya	3.7	−1.7	−19.0
Malawi	3.6	−1.4	−17.0
Rwanda	3.5	−0.3	−4.0
Nigeria	3.3	−0.5	−7.0
Liberia	3.3	−0.4	−5.0
Mali	3.2	−0.4	−5.0
Ethiopia	3.0	−0.9	−11.0
Mozambique	2.7	−5.0	−49.0
Angola	2.8	−5.4	−52.0
Egypt	2.8	−1.5	−18.0

2010, at least eight more countries will join the list. Even ignoring other serious problems of air pollution and other potential climate changes, these are warning signs of potential future food shortages.

All indications are that we will not be able to grow ourselves out of this problem. Time, space, and complexity seem to be against us: time because local problems are becoming regional problems, regional problems are becoming national problems, and national problems are becoming global problems; space because acute problems are becoming chronic problems; complexity because simple problems are becoming complex problems.

All of this suggests that unless human population growth is curbed, there will be too many of us placing demands on resources we think are unlimited but are not. What should we do about this serious problem? The paradox is that we increase the hungry by feeding the hungry. If we have real food shortages in the future, will we let these people starve, or will we accept a decline in our own standard of living to feed these additional people? If it is in our power to prevent something bad from happening and it doesn't cost us something of comparable moral importance, shouldn't we do it? (Singer, 1977). What should we do?

The Case for Agricultural Ethics

This publication represents the thinking of several individuals about the problems of animal welfare, conventional and alternative agriculture, and world hunger. Whether any proposed solutions for these agricultural problems are right or wrong is not as important as talking about them — the sooner, the better. What kind of agriculture do we want? The prospect of world hunger and human survival makes agricultural ethics a compelling issue. What we think *is* important. We need increased sensitivity on the part of agriculture to the entire spectrum of ethical concern, and in particular we need it in our agricultural curricula, where for too long there has been an imbalance — we absorb and apply a body of knowledge but not a method of thought and analysis. In this concern the Tri-Societies should take a leadership role.

References

Albright, J.L. 1983. Status of animal welfare awareness of producers and direction of animal welfare research in the future. J. Dairy Sci. 66:2208–2220.

Bartram, W. 1791. Travels through North & South Carolina, Georgia, East & West Florida, the Cherokee country, the extensive territories of the Muscogulges, or Creek Confederacy, and the country of the Chactaws; containing an account of the soil and natural productions of those regions, together with observations on the manners of the Indians. James & Johnson, Philadelphia.

Berry, W. 1977. The unsettling of America: Culture & agriculture. Sierra Club Books, San Francisco.

Berry, W. 1990. What are people for? North Point Press, San Francisco.

Beus, C.E., R.E. Dunlap, R.M. Jimmerson, and W.L. Holmes. 1991. Competing paradigms: The debate between alternative and conventional agriculture. Res. Bull. XB1020. Washington State Univ., Pullman.

Brown, L.R. 1993. A new era unfolds. p. 3–21. In L.R. Brown et al. (ed.) State of the world, 1993. W.W. Norton & Co., New York.

Carreker, J.R., and A.P. Barnett. 1949. Runoff and soil loss measurements by cropping periods. Agric. Eng. 30:173-176.

Cox, G.W., and M.D. Atkins. 1979. Agricultural ecology. An analysis of world food production systems. W. H. Freeman and Company, San Francisco.

Davion, V. 1994. Where are we headed? p. 1–6. In F. Ferré and P.G. Hartel (ed.) Ethics and environmental policy: Theory meets practice. Univ. of Georgia Press, Athens.

Dundon, S.J. 1991. Sources of first principles for an agricultural ethic. p. 63–74. In C.V. Blatz (ed.) Ethics and agriculture. An anthology on current issues in world context. Univ. of Idaho Press, Moscow.

Duvick, D.N. 1991. Genetic diversity and plant breeding. p. 492–498. In C.V. Blatz (ed.) Ethics and agriculture. An anthology on current issues in world context. Univ. of Idaho Press, Moscow.

Fox, M.W. 1983. Farm animal welfare and the human diet. Humane Soc. United States, Washington, DC.

Hightower, J. 1973. Hard tomatoes, hard times. A report of the Agribusiness Accountibility Project on the failure of America's land grant college complex. Schenkman Publ., Cambridge, MA.

Kaufmann, R. 1993. Opponents set 1993 tactics for animal rights showdown. The Scientist 7(2):1, 6–7.

Madden, P. 1991. Values, economics, and agricultural research. p. 285–298. In C.V. Blatz (ed.) Ethics and agriculture. An anthology on current issues in world context. Univ. of Idaho Press, Moscow.

Postel, S. 1993. Facing water scarcity. p. 22–41. In L.R. Brown et al. (ed.) State of the world, 1993. W.W. Norton & Co., New York.

Shrader-Fréchette, K. 1994. An apologia for activism: Global responsibility, ethical advocacy, and environmental problems. p. 178–194. In F. Ferré and P.G. Hartel (ed.) Ethics and environmental crisis: Theory meets practice. Univ. of Georgia Press, Athens.

Singer, P. 1977. Famine, affluence, and morality. p. 22–36. In J. Rachels (ed.) Moral problems. A collection of philosophical essays. 3rd ed. Harper & Row, New York.

Soil Conservation Service. 1968. Soil survey of Clarke and Oconee counties, Georgia. U.S. Gov. Print. Office, Washington, DC.

Swanson, T. 1991. Conserving biological diversity. p. 181–208. In D. Pearce et al. (ed.) Greening the world's economy. Earthscan Publ. Ltd., London.

Thompson, P.B., R. Matthews, and E. van Ravenswaay. 1994. Ethics, public policy, and agriculture. Macmillan, New York.

Tweeten, L. 1991. Food for people and profit. Ethics and capitalism. p. 84–100. In C.V. Blatz (ed.) Ethics and agriculture. An anthology on current issues in world context. Univ. of Idaho Press, Moscow.

United Nations Population Fund. 1992. The state of world population. Nuffield Press, Oxford, England.

U.S. Department of Agriculture. 1986. World indices of agricultural and food production, 1950–1985. U.S. Gov. Print. Office, Washington, DC.

Wojcik, J. 1989. The arguments of agriculture: A casebook in contemporary agricultural controversy. Purdue Univ. Press, West Lafayette, IN.

World Commission on Environment and Development. 1987. Our common future. Oxford Univ. Press, New York.

Zak, S. 1989. Ethics and animals. Atlantic Monthly 263:69–74.

2 No Hiding Place: The Inescapability of Agricultural Ethics

Frederick Ferré

University of Georgia
Athens, Georgia

I think there are two main reasons for doubt or cynicism about ethics. One is the fact, proven over and over again, that ethical laws are entirely different from scientific laws. Ethical laws (if there are any) are a cinch to break. People do it all the time. And nothing obvious happens. It is easy to see that matters are very different when dealing with a "real" law, like gravity. For two decades I have held a certificate from the FAA authorizing me, as a flight instructor, to try to make the skies safe for would-be defiers of the law of gravity. It takes very little demonstration to bring my flight students to the healthy conviction that thin air is a relentlessly unforgiving environment for human flesh. Our weight remains safely suspended above the earth, if it does, only by our scrupulously obeying Nature's lawful decrees. The laws that science deals with demand obedience; they get respect — or else.

In contrast to my flight students, my ethics students cannot be forced to give ethical laws similar respect. Ethical laws, even if they can be agreed on, are prescriptive, not descriptive. They say what *should* be, not what *must* be or even what *is*. In a word, they are *normative*: asserting a standard or ideal, a goal or principle, not necessarily an actual state of affairs. Knowing the way things are does not tell us what ought to be, any more than knowing what ought to be in theory tells us what is so in fact. If John *is* a greedy liar, that doesn't mean he ought to be; and, vice versa, if America *ought* to be a kinder, gentler place, that doesn't mean it is. Ethics, even at best, can command nothing stronger than moral authority. That will not be my last word on this subject; I shall come back to it at the end, but at this point it should be clear why, for some practical people, ethics does not get much respect.

The second reason for a low regard of ethics is the emotional babble and confusion that surrounds ethical questions when they start to matter. Diametrically opposed views can be held with apparently equally strong conviction; every ethical argument apparently can be met with an equally strong-sounding counter-argument; disputes over ethics seem never to end; and all that comes

Copyright © 1994 American Society of Agronomy, Crop Science Society of America, Soil Science Society of America, 677 S. Segoe Rd., Madison, WI 53711, USA. *Agricultural Ethics: Issues for the 21st Century*, ASA Special Publication no. 57.

from arguing over ethics seems to be anger, division, and sour feelings. There is little wonder, when ethics is seen like this, that intelligent, practical people of good will prefer to avoid getting tarred. Many have dismissed the whole enterprise as ''just opinion'' or ''nothing but feeling.''

In answer to these negative attitudes toward ethics, we had better begin by distinguishing ethical thinking from mere bathing in emotion. There is no doubt that ethical issues get our feelings worked up, but there is a crucial difference between making thoughtful ethical judgments and just spouting off emotions. To prove this difference we need simply remember that feelings and thoughts vary independently of one another. For example, if I witness an act of injustice, I may both judge that it is wrong and, in the heat of the moment, feel very strongly against it. But later, as time passes and my *feelings* fade, my earlier *judgments* need not diminish at all. They may even be strengthened on reflection. Generally, the calming of feeling tends to give thought a better chance. If they were the just the same thing, this could not happen.

Therefore, we have learned one important lesson in approaching ethics, very much including agricultural ethics: we must keep our feelings from clouding our heads. This does not mean that we should deny our moral intuitions or be ashamed of our sense of moral indignation when we judge something to be wrong. These are appropriate for the beginnings and endings of ethical reasoning. But reasoning is really what we are doing when we enter the ethical arena. For this we need to keep clear minds.

If we try to think, not just emote, will we be more likely to overcome the endless contentiousness of what is too often seen as ethical debate? Yes — to a large and important extent we should be able to clarify issues and narrow differences. Many so-called ethical arguments are really not over matters of ''ought'' so much as ''is'': for example, whether the death penalty *is* or *is not* a deterrent. The answers to such factual questions can and ought to be established using standard, impartial investigative procedures. After minds are clear and in good working order, then, the first rule is to get all the relevant facts correct. If the facts are in dispute, good ethical thinking will demand research. That is an empirical job for qualified investigators, not a fit subject for rhetorical posturing. If it turns out that the facts are simply not known by anyone, then these limits of knowledge should be accepted by all sides and alternative hypothetical scenarios discussed while further research proceeds.

A calm, relatively dispassionate spirit and a clear knowledge of the pertinent facts make a good start, but since ethical reasoning is a type of reasoning, we must add good logic as well. This means that in ethical thinking a self-contradiction is just as nullifying of meaning as in any other line of thought. It means that concepts need to be as thoroughly clarified and defined — and pruned of subliminal ''persuaders'' that often come with highly charged topics. If this means that ethical discourse needs to sound a bit dull, so be it; dullness is better than begging questions with words — like ''murder'' instead of ''homicide'' — that convict in the very act of describing.

A homicide may be justifiable; murder is by definition always wrong. Finally, still on the requirement of good logic, to *consistency* and *clarity* we should add *coherence*, so that our ideas not only avoid canceling each other out (that is the essential minimum that consistency assures) but also positively hang together and lead to one another. We want our ethical thought to make sense as a whole. From the judgments we make in one area (e.g., safety protections due migrant workers) we should be able to reason our way to coherent judgments in others (e.g., protections due other easily victimized subjects of moral attention, from Brazilian peasants or generations of Americans yet unborn, to farm animals and fragile soils).

So far I have been talking about attitudinal, factual, and formal requirements for good ethical thinking. They are all areas where people, adequately trained in science and logic, should be able to reach consensus. But what about the goods we seek and the harms we try to avoid? And what about the principles of right and wrong themselves? They seem so fundamental and, being normative rather than descriptive, they are not directly open to factual proof or disproof. Do they condemn ethical thinking to a mere scrimmage between private preferences?

No. Even when we get into the normative substance of ethics we find a surprising degree of consensus among those who try to think carefully and calmly about these matters. Consider what people tend to seek as "good" for themselves and their loved ones. In overwhelming majorities they want to survive; they want good health; they want to be secure from harm and, if possible, to be comfortable; they want to enjoy the stimulation of human society; they want to exercise their own agency, to be self-determining, to enjoy some dignity. People in northern and southern hemispheres alike want these goals; there is nothing esoteric about them. Assuredly, details will differ. What "comfortable" means is always relative to perceived cultural norms, though "health" is much less so. But we are not total strangers to each other. At root our judgments of value and disvalue are intelligible and nonarbitrary.

But of course the goods I have listed are not *moral* goods. Just because someone is healthy and comfortable does not make that person ethically praiseworthy. How that comfort was obtained, and how it is maintained, under the circumstances of others also seeking survival, health, and comfort — these are the distinctly ethical questions for which we have been waiting for. If achieved, were these ends *well-gotten* or *ill-gotten*? The "how" more than the "what" concerns ethical judgments of right and wrong. Is this where ethical reasoning must simply fall apart, foundering on the rocks of irreducibly different principles of conduct?

Even here there is likely to be more consensus than the babble of unthinking zealots would lead us to expect. At bottom, nearly everyone who thinks at all about ethical principle comes to see that fairness (or, more pretentiously, justice) is at the root of right conduct. Fairness, equity, at its most elemental level, is the principle of similar treatment under similar circumstances. In other words, it is the determination not to discriminate without a justification that can withstand objective scrutiny — scrutiny from any neutral point of view, independent of private likes and prejudices. This does not require mathematical equality in the distribution of the goods we all value, but it starts from the presumption of equality and then makes legitimate adjustments. Hence, if I treat myself to a steak dinner but give you only strained spinach for your main course, this might be justified ... if you are a baby. The ethical discussion then focuses, properly, on the reasons that are given for making adjustments. Do they hold up? Could a neutral judge agree? In many cases just getting this question clearly in focus will go a long way toward answering it. Being an infant, having no teeth and an undeveloped digestive system, may be a legitimate ground for discriminations in treatment. Is eye color? Should all steak dinners — or all top executive positions — be reserved for blue-eyed people (like me)? Why or why not? The answer should be clear, even to blue-eyed people, that eye color is irrelevant to the distribution of nonmoral goods that brown-eyed, green-eyed, black-eyed, and grey-eyed people want and can benefit from as much as blue-eyed ones.

Not all questions of this sort are equally obvious, practically answering themselves when they are clearly posed. But asking such questions, even tough ones, calmly and clearly, could help greatly in coming to broader ethical consensus on common policy in agriculture as in other domains of life. What are the *goods* at stake? What are the *principles* reflected in our proposed course of action? How close to *neutrally justifiable* are the reasons we give for diverging from equality in treatment?

Actually doing this takes work and care. There are plenty of places to go astray. One of the most common (and treacherous) ways of getting frustrated in ethical argument, no matter how well intentioned, is to lose track of what, exactly, is being discussed. If I am deeply concerned about maximizing the goods that all or nearly all people want, I may be inclined to harp on that concern to the exclusion of all interest in the means by which these ends are achieved. If you, conversely, are intensely worried that the principle of my action might be unfair, you might very well want to slow me down in my quest for the *good* by insisting single-mindedly that it is not *right*. And both of us could be correct!

One school of thought in ethics takes the achievement of the good to be the only thing that counts. I shall call it *aim ethics,* since it insists that only the outcome of an action should count in determining its ethical value. To figure out what one should do, in this view of ethics, one must always look to the future results.

Another school of thought takes the principle of the action as the only thing that matters. I shall call it *rule ethics* since it argues that only following the right rule, doing one's duty in principle, whatever the consequences, can allow correct ethical decisions.

These two schools tend, unfortunately, to talk past one another rather than to one another. We see this illustrated in the debate over the question of capital punishment. The opposition may emphasize the irreversible consequences of taking a life when proof of innocence is always possible; the pro-capital-punishment side may offer the principle of retribution, "an eye for an eye." Or, the other way around, the supporting side may claim relief of jail overcrowding and predict deterrence; the opposition may reply, "Thou shalt not kill." When this happens, the two sides merely talk past one another and so never really come to grips with the other's points. Rule arguments, deduced from principle, need to be met by thoughtful discussions of conflicting principles and how they might be resolved by appeals to still higher principles. Aim arguments about probable consequences must be evaluated by well-informed examination of known facts about the probable future. Once this difference between aims for the future and respect for rules is clearly seen, there may be more hope of sorting out some of these controversial matters. That hope is practically important, since civilized recourse to ethical rationality is itself caught in the crossfire when the public is unaware that shouting at cross purposes is not the only way of dealing with ethical disagreement.

There is, indeed, a better way. And once the better is seen as available, it becomes obligatory. Thinking, after all, is one of the things we *do*. Like everything else we do, thinking can be done well or poorly, and ethical thinking is no exception. To put it bluntly: as rational beings who act, we are under moral obligation to seek maximum ethical clarity as we make ethically significant decisions. If we allow ourselves to remain blinded in some emotional dust storm, or — even worse! — if we contribute to raising the dust by our own puffery, we are literally doing wrong.

It does no good to say that we will protect our innocence by not making decisions. In many cases, not making a decision is actually making a decision by default. If a farmer can't make a decision whether he should plant a certain field and keeps postponing the decision, he or she has obviously made the decision not to plant. Many ethical questions, usually called *forced options,* are like that. Shall I blow the whistle on some injustice I see? Not deciding is deciding to take the easy way out — and offers no escape from responsibility for the default decision. Shall I return the extra change the cashier gave me by mistake? Not deciding is deciding to keep what doesn't belong to me. Shall I subject this upcoming decision to calm and searching ethical scrutiny? Not deciding to think my best is deciding to let other pressures and interests make the decision for me. And just as there is such a thing as "culpable ignorance" in courts of law, so likewise there is such a thing as "negligent thinking" in daily decisions. This is what I mean in my title by "no hiding place." Once you know a better way, you are under an obligation to follow it — or show that there is a still better way. But showing this would itself be following the better way of ethically self-aware, calm, clear, factually accurate, and logically valid reasoning. There truly is no ethical escape from ethics.

This is particularly important to realize when it comes to agricultural decision-making. Agricultural questions are perfect examples of forced options. People must eat. Food must be produced one way or another. Animals, soil, and water must be treated in the process. There is no escaping these decisions, and postponing them is in effect deciding to go along with the status quo.

For all of the above reasons, ready or not, agricultural ethics is here to stay. We are no longer morally free to let the status quo continue — or be changed — without thoughtful ethical examination. What are the appropriate ethical principles for future agricultural decisions? What are their probable consequences? These questions press us now and will continue to press ever more heavily as we move into the 21st century, a century in which populations are sure to wax and arable land to wane.

Fortunately, in my view, aims for achieving maximum good can still be harmonized with rules for just distribution. I would go further: they need each other. Maximum sustainable yield of food and fiber depends in the long run — for the 21st century and beyond — on the maintenance of worldwide social order. That alone will make possible the huge worldwide cooperative efforts needed for such good consequences to be achieved in fact. But worldwide social order depends on the nurture and advancement of real justice and on the perception of justice in principle. Shared benefits, shared sacrifices around the interconnected globe are required. This is as true in principle as it is necessary in practice. Any agricultural ethics for the 21st century must begin here.

The sanctions against violating ethical rules, as I noted at the outset, are not at all like those that punish our trying to defy scientific laws. We can only *illustrate* the laws of nature, even when we are foolish enough to try to break them, but we can easily *violate* the laws of ethics. And, as I said above, nothing obvious happens. We may seem to get away with it. The wicked, as the Psalmist complained, seem to flourish. But does this seeming escape from consequences hold true for fundamental human choices, as in the matter of bringing forth and distributing food from the earth? Does it hold true over the long run? I think not. Meeting long-term human needs demands sustainability; sustainability over the long run requires justice. Without doing *right* we cannot long maintain the *good*.

I finish, then, with a glimpse of this truth for the 21st century through "Calvin and Hobbes," the cartoon by Bill Waterson (Universal Press Syndicate, 26 July 1992). Calvin tests the ethical character of the universe in this sequence, as he fills his balloon with water and prepares to douse his friend Susie. "In order to determine if there is any universal moral law beyond human convention, I have devised the following test," he says. "I will throw this water balloon at Susie Derkins unless I receive some sign within the next 30 seconds that this is wrong." He waits, with upraised eyes. "It is in the universe's power to stop me," he promises. "I'll accept any remarkable physical happenstance as a sign that I shouldn't do this. Ready? Go!" He waits his 30 seconds. Nothing happens. "Time's up! That proves it! There's no moral law!

Wheee!'' And with that he smashes his water balloon all over Susie. Next frame: the outraged, dripping Susie chases Calvin with baleful intent. Finally, at the end, Calvin is found lying in a broken heap, musing sadly, ''Why does the universe always give you the sign *after* you do it?''

To avoid that sad query at the end of the 21st century is the practical importance of agricultural ethics. To outrage the universe is possible, but not wise. We can run from our responsibilities as moral agents but we cannot hide. Like it or not, ready or not, the age of agricultural ethics has arrived.

3 Farm Animal Welfare: Obligations, Realities, and Compromises

Stanley E. Curtis

The Pennsylvania State University
University Park, Pennsylvania

Otto von Bismarck, Germany's Iron Chancellor, remarked more than a century ago, "Laws are like sausages; it is better not to watch them being made." I am afraid much the same could be said today about agricultural animals in the USA. Most of our fellow citizens are so far removed from animal production agriculture in their experience, let alone everyday life, that they are turned off by it. An aesthetic aversion, if you will. But after all, life is accompanied by messy sights and unpleasant smells, and it always will be.

Unfamiliarity with animal production seems to have led some to question everything farmers do as they keep and care for agricultural animals. Some of these people most sensitive to the feelings of animals feel free to criticize and disparage practices they do not understand (Mason and Singer, 1990). The image problem of contemporary agriculture related to the well-being of animals on farms and ranches keeps the animal welfare issue on state and national agendas. While a recent poll conducted by the National Cattlemen's Association in the USA shows that two-thirds of the respondents believe that farm animals are being treated humanely, the respondents also want federal regulations for the care of farm animals (now state laws regulate animal care on farms). Representative Charles Stenholm (Democrat–TX), the immediate past chair of the House Agriculture Subcommittee on Livestock, Dairy, and Poultry, expects that legislation will be passed by the year 2000 requesting the Department of Agriculture to establish such regulations and enforce them. The potential ramifications for all of agriculture — and certainly the forages, pastures, and feed grains sectors — are great indeed. Robert McDowell (1991) concluded that "85% or more of the world's total farms (if pastoralists are included) are dependent on animals as a means of bridging the gap[s][among] cropping, total food needs, and minimal income," and moreover that "cessation of the role of animals in land and risk management would be catastrophic on a global scale." Shall we explore briefly the roots of this public, ethical issue — farm animal welfare?

Copyright © 1994 American Society of Agronomy, Crop Science Society of America, Soil Science Society of America, 677 S. Segoe Rd., Madison, WI 53711, USA. *Agricultural Ethics: Issues for the 21st Century*, ASA Special Publication no. 57.

"Animals in service of humankind," some say about agricultural animal production. We might also say humans in service of the animals. On a tapestry in the auditorium of the veterinary school in Utrecht, the Netherlands, appear the words of the Dutch poet, P.C. Boutens: "We serve, in never fulfilled repayment, the animals that accompany humankind." McDowell (1991) reminds us of this partnership, this relationship we humans have with nonhuman animals. They serve us and we serve them. We benefit from them and they benefit from us. So it has been for more than 10 000 years.

Then why the hullabaloo? Why the protests? Why the charges that we humans are exploiting nonhuman animals? Why the terrorism on behalf of animals against humans who use animals in various ways?

Some reasons probably are due to simple ignorance of the details of the partnership between humans and animals. Others may have their origins in a privileged human standard of living and the guilt this can engender. Still others, more than anything else, are probably due to simple human nature.

Six months ago, a rational, rhetorical question to ask would have been: "Why did humans domesticate animals in the first place?" And then I could well have gone on to detail the conventional wisdom of archeologists and anthropologists of the last 200 years: agricultural development started with the New Stone Age around 17 000 years before present. Cave dwellers and hunters and gatherers became farmers. Through a sequence of human-centered relationships, humans and animals came together, and so on (Zeuner, 1963; Serpell, 1986).

But now comes Stephen Budiansky's book, *The Covenant of the Wild*, with its intriguing subtitle: *Why Animals Chose Domestication* (1991). And Budiansky urges us to reconsider conventional notions of how domestication occurred. To quote him: " ... [T]he first chore for anyone who would set out to prove that the domestication of animals is a natural product of evolution is to undo several thousand years of human self-importance." He goes on to say, "It is a central myth of our culture that we are firmly in control of our destiny."

Well! Pretty strong words this fellow has for us agricultural scientists, has he not? All along we thought we were succeeding in our quest to control nature, to subdue nature, to make nature over to fit our notions and meet our needs. Be that as it may, Budiansky makes this point:

> The only way to produce an animal with the desirable traits is through captive breeding, yet the only way they could have been captively bred is if they had the desirable traits to start with. This paradox is the crux of the entire, counterintuitive line of evidence that argues for domestication as an evolutionary, rather than a human, invention. The only way out is to recognize that, in an evolutionary sense, domesticated animals chose us as much as we chose them.

There is a lesson here vis-à-vis radical animal activism. For eons, these animals, which we use and care for in return, have been unusual creatures. Even before they were domesticated, they were special. That is an important reason why they became domesticated in the first place. They were useful to us, to be sure. But first and foremost, they were adaptable, for their own sakes, and they wanted access to human resources.

In today's world, the animals that accompany humankind are virtually indispensable. If animal use were to stop now absolutely, a very different world would need to be developed, and fast! In the first place, humans around the globe need animals for food — eggs, meat, and milk — especially so in the developing parts of the world. To quote McDowell again (1991): "Cessation of the role of animals in land and risk management would be catastrophic on a global scale." The animals that at first simply started "hanging around" our ancestors have come to be managed by humans to provide a plethora of goods and services.

Are we exploiting animals as we use them? I suggest that we are not. To exploit is "to make use of meanly or unjustly for one's own advantage." On the one hand, animal rights advocates believe that "a rat is a dog is a pig is a boy," that animals have rights, that the primary right an animal possesses is the right not be used in any way whatsoever by a human being. In philosophy, the rights argument is an all-or-none, trump-card approach. On the other hand, most people hold that we do have the right to use animals for our own advantage — as long as that use is "neither mean nor unjust." Animal welfarists, both those involved in the social movement and those who use animals in various ways, believe that we humans may use animals for whatever purpose, but that we have an obligation to ensure the well-being of those animals that we use.

Today, we in the mainstream of animal use are searching for the line that separates wellness from illness in the animals we use. We are obliged to find that line and then to abide by it. The search for that line by scientists from a variety of disciplines has turned out to be a difficult undertaking. Alas, it does not suffice to simply gather a panel of experts, give them a piece of chalk, and direct them to draw that line. Today, we simply do not know for sure where to draw that line or what criteria to use, and no amount of armchair musing, philosophizing, sympathizing, or moralizing is going to be of much help.

To paraphrase Boutens, what we must do to fulfill our obligation to the animals that accompany us is to serve them. In my opinion we serve them best when we attempt to determine how they feel. The tools of cognitive psychology are ready and waiting for us to apply to finding out how animals feel in any given environment or situation. It is only a matter of time until we learn how animals feel — how they consciously perceive their environments and experiences (Duncan and Petherick, 1991). When we do find that line, can anyone imagine not wanting to honor it? But maybe it is not as simple as this, after all. That line — the one that separates wellness from illness in the animals we use — probably does not provide for maximal comfort of the animal. Some people will want to see the animals in quarters better than the minimally acceptable. But does an animal truly need such in order to meet its basic needs? In order to be well? In order to experience well-being? By definition, the answer is "no."

It is axiomatic that, when an animal's needs are not being met, the animal is not as well as it could be. Its welfare is more or less jeopardized. But here we must remember that a particular decrement in well-being does not necessarily mean that the animal is residing in an ethically unacceptable environment. Perhaps the animal simply experiences less — but still an ethically acceptable amount — of well-being.

On any farm, consistently achieving the highest level of animal well-being possible is still a vague exercise, and in my opinion it probably will be so for several years. C.D. Hardwick of the United Kingdom formulated the idea that an ethically acceptable level of animal well-being exists across a range of environmental conditions provided by a variety of agricultural production systems, not only in one set of circumstances called *ideal*. Hardwick (according to Duncan, 1978) envisioned what he called the *welfare plateau*. On the welfare plateau, a relatively small environmental change might subtly improve an animal's overall well-being, but everywhere on the welfare plateau the animal is as free from suffering as possible (Curtis, 1987). But this concept has not caught on, probably because Hardwick presented it abstractly, and we have difficulty identifying the limits. Perhaps we should refer instead to surroundings that might be called "minimal ethically acceptable conditions" (MEAC). True, a relatively small improvement in the environment might enhance — even if only subtly — an animal's overall well-being, but nevertheless in MEAC the animal is as free from suffering as possible.

The farmer as businessperson recognizes that, in MEAC, the economic law of diminishing returns works. Returns to investments in environmental improvements are not sufficient to pay for the improvements. In the range of unacceptable conditions, however, small improvements in the environment result in returns that are more than adequate to pay for the improvements. This is because well-being and productivity are directly linked. Therefore, perhaps to the dismay of some of the more strident animal activists, there is a tendency for the most widely adopted production systems to be located at the level of MEAC — and no higher.

For the sake of economic viability, the farmer is faced with the necessity of compromising maximal animal well-being. To locate production environments nearer the humane ideal would be an unwise business decision; as long as the adopted production system is within the range of MEAC, the farmer's ethical obligations have been satisfied.

To conclude, animal agriculture faces a dilemma. Farmers must decide on animal production systems, constrained by humane concerns of their own as well as those of the consumers on the one hand, and by the realities of doing business in a free-enterprise climate on the other. This dilemma will be resolved only if and when we learn more than we know now about animal well-being and production environments that fall within the range of MEAC.

So it is that a public issue such as farm animal welfare benefits from inputs of agricultural scientists. In a democracy, I believe that economics, ethics, and aesthetics should operate from the soundest factual base possible.

References

Budiansky, S. 1992. The covenant of the wild: Why animals chose domestication. William Morrow, New York.

Curtis, S.E. 1985. What constitutes well-being? p. 1–14. *In* G.P. Moberg (ed.) Animal stress. Am. Physiol. Soc., Bethesda, MD.

Curtis, S.E. 1987. The case for intensive farming of food animals. p. 245–255. *In* M.W. Fox and L.D. Mickley (ed.) Advances in animal welfare science. Martinus Nijhoff Publ., Boston.

Duncan, I.J.H. 1978. An overall assessment of poultry welfare. p. 81–87. *In* L.Y. Sorensen (ed.) Proc. Danish seminar on poultry welfare in egglaying cages 1st. Køge, Denmark. 30–31 Aug. 1978. Natl. Committee for Poultry and Eggs, Copenhagen.

Duncan, I.J.H., and J.C. Petherick. 1991. The implications of cognitive processes for animal welfare. J. Anim. Sci. 69:5017–5022.

Mason, J., and P. Singer. 1990. Animal factories. Harmony Books, New York.

McDowell, R.E. 1991. A partnership for humans and animals. Kinnic Publ., Raleigh, NC.

Serpell, J. 1986. In the company of animals: A study of human–animal relationships. Basil Blackwell, Oxford, England.

Zeuner, F.E. 1963. A history of domesticated animals. Harper and Row, New York.

4

Some Virtues and Vices of Agricultural Technology

Gary Comstock

Iowa State University
Ames, Iowa

The secret workings of nature do not reveal themselves to one who simply contemplates the natural flow of events. It is when nature is tormented by art, when man interferes with nature, vexes nature, tries to make her do what he wants, not what she wants, that he begins to understand how she works and may hope to learn how to control her. ... It is my intention to bind, and place at your command, nature ...

— Francis Bacon (Farrington, 1949)

Humanity cannot afford to acknowledge all of the blood that it spills and the destruction it inflicts on the world in its effort to perpetuate itself ... [and place nature] under our control ...

— Jeremy Rifkin (1983)

What has Francis Bacon to do with the Tri-Societies? He articulates their very reason for being: to learn how to control nature's prairies and make her grasslands produce food and fiber for us. Bacon declared his intent around 1600 and, in the 400 intervening years, agronomists, soil scientists, and crop specialists have learned so much about the natural flow of events that they have given us by far the most productive agriculture in history. They have not only helped us to learn how nature works, but through technology have bound her, placed her at our command, and made her produce more corn, soybeans, wheat, and oats per hectare than she ever could have produced without them. As the saying goes, never before have so few fed so many.

Few figures in the history of science are bigger than Sir Francis Bacon. Then why taint the memory of a hero by bringing into his vicinity that villain of modern science than whom none worse can be imagined? Because Jeremy Rifkin provides one reason the Tri-Societies are sponsoring discussions of agricultural ethics. Agronomists, soil scientists, and crop scientists are increasingly aware of the potentially negative effects of modern agricultural technologies on soil, wildlife, farm families, and rural communities. Members

Copyright © 1994 American Society of Agronomy, Crop Science Society of America, Soil Science Society of America, 677 S. Segoe Rd., Madison, WI 53711, USA. *Agricultural Ethics: Issues for the 21st Century*, ASA Special Publication no. 57.

of the Tri-Societies do not need to be told that our culture has not paid the external environmental costs of modern agriculture, and we do not need Rifkin to tell us there are hidden social and cultural costs from technologies that reduce the demand for farm labor and move families out of farming. We know that. What we need to know is: How do we decide what is good and bad in agricultural technology?

Military machines, distrustful people, and unending wars in the 20th century have been responsible for unparalleled destruction. But Rifkin implies that agriculture, that most peaceful of occupations, should be held responsible for bloodshed. Agriculture? Aren't agricultural technologies proverbially created *out of* the swords of hatred, when the implements of war are beaten into the plowshares of peace? Of course they are. One reason agricultural scientists are beginning to think about ethics is that they know that in the past some of the costs of our amazing productivity have been hidden, and sooner or later someone will have to pay for them.

Bacon or Rifkin: How do we decide who is right? To answer this question we must first address a more fundamental one, and that is, what are the criteria by which we should assess the moral virtues and vices of agricultural technology? To assess this is a bit like trying to decide whom to choose next for your pick-up basketball game. You first have to decide what you need and what your aims are before you can make up your mind about whom to select for your team. Once you've picked two players, someone is sure to disagree with you about whom to pick next. Do you need a shooter, a ball handler, a rebounder, a defensive star, or a role player (that is, someone you can count on to stay out of your way)? A basketball player's skills can be virtues or vices depending on the opponent and the goals of the team. Analogously, an agricultural technology can be a virtue or a vice depending on which other technologies are currently in place, in which political, economic, and ecological context these technologies are operating, and the goals of agriculture. To decide whether a particular agricultural technology is morally good or bad, we must first decide what we have, what we need, where we are, and where we want to go.

If we believe that we are in good shape overall, that the current agricultural system is a good one, that new technologies ought to be aimed at achieving further increments in production efficiency, then we will want to choose technologies that substitute lower cost genetics, machines, and capital for higher cost labor and land. With these goals in mind, new agricultural biotechnologies such as genetically engineered herbicide-resistant crops, bovine somatotropin, Ice-Minus strawberries, and Flavr-Savr tomatoes will appear to be good choices, virtues.

There are indeed good reasons to think that these technologies *are* virtues, the most obvious being that the current set of technologies feeds millions. With our tractors and combines, high-yielding seed varieties and synthetic fertilizers, herbicides and pesticides, cash crops and export markets, modern Baconian agriculture has not only provided huge quantities of nutritious food to hungry people, but it has enabled us to reduce the amount of money we spend on food and fiber. Real food prices have declined dramatically during the last century. In 1891, Americans spent about 40% of their income on food; today that figure is roughly 15%. Modern agriculture has also allowed us to cut the amount of on-farm labor needed to produce food. In 1910, the number of hours of labor required to produce a bushel of corn was 50 times as great as it is today. What is more, choices for consumers have multiplied. In 1941, there were some 1500 different food items in grocery stores. Today that figure is closer to 15 000 (Lee and Taylor, 1986). How exactly did this happen? How have we managed to reduce expenditures on food while increasing choices? It is because we have invested heavily in agricultural research and development. In the USA, yields of corn and soybean have tripled during the present century. According to Gary Jolliff (1989), about 50% of this increase can be attributed to the work of plant breeders alone. Here are some persuasive reasons to think that our team is in good shape and to believe that our next technologies should complement and continue the institutions and practices currently in place.

But not everyone on the team agrees. Some think our team is in worse shape than we believe. The critics of biotechnology do not think we need more and better technologies. They think we need to change the fundamental goals of agriculture, and move from petrochemically based agriculture to ecologically based agriculture. With world population continuing to expand, it would be irrational to renounce utterly the goal of increased production efficiency. Is it rational to believe we can feed (on a prolonged basis) twice the number of people currently living, simply by doing more of what we have been doing? If one is inclined to doubt our ability to double food production in the next 50 years, Baconian agriculture will no longer seem unblemished and pure. Indeed, F. Gregory Hayden, professor of economics at the University of Nebraska, described our system rather differently from the way it is described in pamphlets put out by the U.S. Department of Agriculture. Hayden (1984) writes that American agriculture is

> an international agribusiness that ... destroys topsoil and water supplies; poisons ground and surface water supplies with chemicals, pesticides, and fertilizers; augments desertification; destroys soil humus and porosity, which means less water retention, which means that compacted soil needs larger tractors which further compact soil; leaches nutrients from and adds salts to the soil through irrigation; uses more energy than it produces; creates worker sterility in the fertilizer factories; creates health problems for farmers who apply the toxic fertilizers, pesticides, and herbicides; uses fertilizers which prevent plants from absorbing nutrients necessary for human health; fills the food chain with carcinogenic pesticides, herbicides, growth hormones, and antibiotics; creates an expensive and unnecessary transportation system; ... processes the nutrients out of what food is produced, with the profits being greater the greater the amount of processing; and fills the processed product with carcinogenic preservatives, refined sugars, salt, and artificial colors.

Hayden is not a lonely voice crying out in the wilderness. His view is shared by a wide range of critics.

Are the Rifkins and Haydens right? Are they the ones we want deciding which technologies to pursue? Your answer will depend on your response to a more fundamental question: How serious are our ecological and communal problems? In answering this question, consider five points.

1. Agricultural activities have vexed nature's soils. To produce a ton of grain at the beginning of this century required virtually no consumption of fossil fuels, and production methods added little pollution to the atmosphere. Today the situation is different. As Lester Brown of the World Watch Institute explains, "On the average, the world's farmers [now] use the equivalent of more than a barrel of oil to produce a ton of grain. Each year it takes more" (*Des Moines Register*, 24 Apr. 1988). Burning fossil fuels produces CO_2, perhaps the leading cause of global warming. Conventional tillage systems, combined with monocultures of corn, have conspired to rob Iowa of 50% of its most precious resource: soil. In the Corn Belt, Baconian methods of raising corn entail a loss by wind, rain, and sheet erosion of 20 t ha^{-1} of soil, or 2.3 bushels of soil for every bushel of corn harvested (Lovins et al., 1984). It is difficult to put an economic figure on this loss, but some agricultural economists have estimated the loss to be worth $4 per ton (Cain, 1991). Hans Jenny (1984) illustrated how extractive these farming methods are:

> Under average farming conditions, over one-third (35 percent) of the nitrogen and carbon content [of previously undisturbed American soils] had been eliminated in the first fifty years [of plow agriculture]. In a prairie soil in Missouri, the actual loss in humus amounted to thirty-one tons per hectare.

2. In addition to vexing nature's soils, we have vexed her plant and animal diversity. As Edward Wilson (1988) notes, tropical rainforests are being razed with chain saws at the annual rate of an area the size of West Virginia in order to raise crops or food animals. The single most important cause in the extinction of species is loss of wildlife habitat. The single most important cause in the loss of wildlife habitat is the enclosure of lands for agricultural production or grazing. Wilson (1988) points out that tropical rainforests

> cover only 7 percent of the Earth's land surface, [but] they contain more than half the species in the entire world biota. ... [They] are being destroyed so rapidly that they will mostly disappear within the next century ... [perhaps by the year 2135], close to the date (2150) that the World Bank has estimated the human population will plateau at 11 billion people.

Genetic diversity is decreasing in both the plant and animal kingdoms as more agricultural production is industrialized, concentrated in the hands of a few producers, and dominated by the interests of large corporations in the farm supply and processing sectors. For particularly vivid examples, think of the loss of farm animal species diversity in the poultry, swine, and dairy industries. All are moving swiftly toward a genetic base of breeding stock that is dangerously narrow, in part because producers work increasingly on large volume and slim profit margins, and in part because they rely on a decreasing number of influential companies for their stock (*Des Moines Register*, 26 Apr. 1992). The Holstein dairy cow has almost completely eclipsed the other breeds, largely because milk pricing policy in the USA rewards high productivity, and because public policy gives comparative advantages to farmers who purchase inexpensive concentrated feeds compared with farmers who rely on grass forages. What does this have to do with *technology*? One reason we are losing diversity on our farms is that agricultural technology, like all technology, is not neutral. It does not arrive naked but arrives in the garb of the worldview that makes it intelligible and useful. Therefore, technology is inherently political, and agricultural politics is heavily influenced by powerful lobbies and commodity groups in Washington. Agricultural policy is not the populist, democratic activity it once was, and the range of choices open to my great-grandfather (choices about which crops to grow, which animals to breed, and which buyers to sell to) is no longer open to my uncle. Self-determination at the local farmer level seems to be vanishing.

3. Contemporary agriculture is directed excessively toward animal products as its end point. We have learned, some of us the hard way, that a diet high in fat, animal protein, and cholesterol leads to an increased risk of various cancers and heart disease. In the average American's diet, almost half of our calories come from fat. Consequently, a diet of meat, milk, eggs, and cheese results in higher public health care costs. We ought to cut our fat intake to no more than a third — better yet, a tenth — of our calories. To do so would be to treat animal products as garnishes for meals at best, certainly not as the main course. Of course, in the present system, more than 70% of the grain grown in this country goes for animal feed. The rate of conversion for grain protein into animal protein is at best 3:1, and more commonly 10:1 or worse, as when corn is fed to beef cattle. Redirecting agriculture toward grains, legumes, and vegetables grown for direct human consumption would not only lead to healthier people and lower health care costs, but would also open up hectares for potential reconversion into wildlife habitat. Human health and biodiversity are good reasons to reduce our use of animals in agriculture. There is another reason: our obligation to respect the basic interests of all sentient animals. I believe most farm animal species have a right to life.

4. Agriculture is increasingly implicated in an inflexible political and economic structure. As I mentioned above, a farmer's choice of which crops to produce, like a young agronomist's choice of which crops to research, is now heavily influenced by governmental support programs. Special-interest farm groups and corporations lobby Congress and woo land-grant university scientists for research funds and price supports for their favorite commodities. Meanwhile, alternative grain crops such as Meadow foam (*Limnanthes* sp. R. Br.) go wanting for sponsors, scientists, and growers.

5. Baconian agriculture is a capital intensive, high volume, low margin, decreasing cost industry. This means that a farmer must be constantly vigilant for ways to increase land holdings in order to spread the costs of machinery and seeds over more hectares. One result is lower food prices. Another is fewer farmers in developing and developed countries. In Egypt, for example, the modernization of agriculture has resulted in more landless farmers now than ever before. In the USA, some 235 000 farms went out of business between 1980 and 1986 (Goldsmith et al., 1992). As farmers go under, rural communities are strained, and the quality of life declines for everyone. Therefore, technology is not only inherently political, it is also inherently moral. Morally, it can be virtuous or vicious depending on whether one counts its costs as "necessary structural adjustments" (or "the price of progress"), or as unfair burdens placed on people who may not share the benefits. In developed countries, growing economies might eventually absorb all displaced farmers back into the job market. In developing countries, however, displaced peasants may find themselves in the slums of Mexico City or São Paolo, perhaps never again to regain their independence and dignity.

Let me put these five problems with modern agriculture into a broader perspective. Net primary production is the conversion of light energy into organic molecules via photosynthesis. When one species begins to capture more than its share of net primary production, other species are denied the resources they need. According to Paul Ehrlich (1988),

> the human share of the ... net primary production reaches almost 40 percent. There is no way that the co-option by one species [out of a total of 1.4 million species] of almost two-fifths of the Earth's annual terrestrial food production could be considered reasonable, in the sense of maintaining the stability of life on this planet. ... (If, as expected, we double our population by 2050, we will need to commandeer a total of 80 percent of terrestrial net primary production, a preposterous notion to ecologists who already see the deadly impacts of today's level of human activities).

Ehrlich provides a vivid image for what is happening: "Earth's habitats are being nickeled and dimed to death ..." He gives this explanation for why we have such a difficult time seeing what we are doing:

> Human beings have great difficulty perceiving and reacting to changes that occur on a scale of decades. Our nervous systems evolved to respond to short-term crises — the potential loss of a mate to a rival, the sudden appearance of a bear in the mouth of a cave. For most of evolutionary history there was no reason for natural selection to tune us to easily recognize more gradual trends, since there was little or nothing we could do about them.

Ehrlich writes that our only answer must be global and spiritual: "Curiously, scientific analysis points toward the need for a quasi-religious transformation of contemporary values." If he is right, then technology is not only intrinsically political and moral; it is intrinsically spiritual as well. By deciding to use and throw away plastic pesticide containers, we are implicitly declaring a certain spiritual attitude toward the earth and toward future generations who will have to deal with our residue. The Amish implicitly declare a very different spiritual attitude toward the value of farming for their children and their children's children. Technology is spiritual, and we ignore its religious significance at our peril.

If the Bacon-esque advocates of modern agriculture are right, then our choices are relatively obvious. We should invest more heavily in technologies that improve production efficiency. But if the Rifkin-esque critics of modern agriculture are right, then our choices are harder. I want to make two suggestions. The first is that we all become more active in the political process and participate in directing the future of agricultural research. Here is the advice of Jack Kloppenburg (1988), sociologist at the University of Wisconsin:

> We must demand more than veto power over technologies and more than the right to regulate technologies. We must demand a role in shaping the very conception and development of new technologies. Those who are affected by economic and technical decisions should be able to participate in those decisions. ... [We need more] sustainable agriculture programs ... such as the Center for Integrated Agricultural Systems at the University of Wisconsin and the Leopold Center at Iowa State University. Such programs are providing a counterbalance to biotechnology with their emphasis on the recovery of historic examples of sustainable agriculture, their explorations of new versions of sustainable practices, their initiatives in farmer participatory research, and their concern for public oversight.

The second suggestion is that we add some truly visionary new players to our roster, in order to achieve a sustainable and humane agriculture. I nominate Wes Jackson, director of The Land Institute in Salina, KS, and a recent recipient of a MacArthur "Genius" prize. Jackson (1991) writes:

> ... At The Land Institute in Salina, Kansas, we have consulted the genius of the place and have devoted time, thought and resources to using nature — in our case native prairie — for biological agriculture. We want to mimic the prairie in vegetative structure. ... [We sort] above-ground plant material into groups of cool and warm season grasses, legumes, sunflowers, family members and other. By knowing how the various ratios for these major plant groups differ across soil types and in wet and dry years, in combination with our data derived from soil–root interactions, we have set out to roughly mimic the native structure with four of our selected perennials. These perennial species are still undergoing germplasm evaluation as we breed for high seed yield and resistance to problems such as seed shatter and pests.

I conclude that if the critics are right in their reading of modern agriculture, then new agricultural biotechnologies such as herbicide-resistant crops and Flavr-Savr tomatoes are not inherently bad. In the short run, they will help us improve the efficiency of a petrochemically based agricultural system. This improved efficiency is a long way from being the only goal we ought to be pursuing, however, and these biotechnologies may be a long way from the technologies we need to help us win the game we are currently playing. At the end of his recent article on growth hormones, Colin Tudge (1991) cited an old Irish saying: "If I was going there, I wouldn't start from here." It is appropriate advice for those thinking seriously about the virtues and vices of agricultural technology.

References

Cain, S. 1991. The wisdom of Solomon. Soybean Dig. 51(6):36–37.

Ehrlich, P.R. 1988. The loss of diversity: Causes and consequences. p. 21–27. In E.O. Wilson (ed.) Biodiversity. Natl. Academy Press, Washington, DC.

Farrington, B. 1949. Francis Bacon, philosopher of industrial science. Henry Schuman, New York.

Goldsmith, E., N. Hildyard, P. Bunyard, and P. McCully. 1992. Whose common future? A special issue. The Ecologist 22(4):144.

Hayden, F.G. 1984. A geobased national agricultural policy for rural community enhancement, environmental vitality, and income stabilization. J. Econ. Issues 18:181–221.

Jackson, W. 1991. Our vision for the agricultural sciences need not include biotechnology. J. Agric. Environ. Ethics 4:200–206.

Jenny, H. 1984. The making and unmaking of a fertile soil. p. 42–55. In W. Jackson et al. (ed.) Meeting the expectations of the land. Essays in sustainable agriculture and stewardship. North Point Press, San Francisco.

Jolliff, G.D. 1989. Strategic planning for new-crop development. J. Prod. Agric. 2:6–13.

Kloppenburg, J.R., Jr. 1988. First the seed: The political economy of plant biotechnology, 1492–2000. Cambridge Univ. Press, New York.

Lee, J.E., Jr., and G.C. Taylor. 1986. Agricultural research: Who pays and who benefits? p. 16–17. In J.C. Crowley (ed.) Research for tomorrow: 1986 Yearbook of agriculture. U.S. Gov. Print. Office, Washington, DC.

Lovins, A.B., L.H. Lovins, and M. Bender. 1984. Energy and agriculture. p. 68–86. In W. Jackson et al. (ed.) Meeting the expectations of the land. Essays in sustainable agriculture and stewardship. North Point Press, San Francisco.

Rifkin, J. 1983. Algeny. Viking Press, New York.

Tudge, C. 1991. Growth hormone biotech and the environment. p. 265–272. In P. van der Wal et al. (ed.) Biotechnology for control of growth and product quality in meat production: Implications and acceptability. PUDOC, Wageningen, the Netherlands.

Wilson, E.O. 1988. The current state of biological diversity. p. 3–18. In E.O. Wilson (ed.) Biodiversity. Natl. Academy Press, Washington, DC.

5   Coming Full Circle: Ethical Issues In Traditional and Industrialized Agriculture

Charles V. Blatz

University of Toledo
Toledo, Ohio

Recent reports suggest that billions of people in the world could be fed with the food produced by the new wonder cultivars of industrialized agriculture (Avery, 1985; Easterbrook, 1985; Duvick, 1991). At the same time, other reports suggest that industrialized agriculture is not sustainable because of its impact on the world's resources and the health and economic well-being of its producers (Strange, 1988; Blatz, 1992). Unlike some traditional agricultures, industrialized agriculture threatens the biological well-being of soil in ways that limit its productive life and serve to drive farmers out of business.

We seem confronted with a choice that is both morally and logically impossible. Morally, how can we choose between the productivity needed to feed the world today and the sustainability needed to feed the world tomorrow? Logically, how can we meaningfully compare, let alone choose between, traditional and industrialized agriculture when they seem to belong to different worlds, when they seem to be cultural and economic apples and oranges? Is there a single standard by which we could assess both traditional and industrialized agriculture and see ways in which each might draw on features of the other to meet common goals? I believe there is, and I want to sketch this common standard and to suggest how it will bring traditional and industrialized agriculture to resemble each other.

Traditional agriculture, as I write of it here, is a freely chosen (or accepted) way of life that allows self-realization, conserves resources, and provides subsistence. Living this way allows people to be family members, parents, conservationists, farmers, and profit seekers. Traditional agriculture, however, is not only a means to one or another of these ends but also a defining framework of agriculture-centered work, recreation, and related activities. In addition, traditional agriculturalists produce food and fiber in ways that were developed by earlier practitioners, *and* they seek to pass on these same or related traditions to future practioners. Although they may believe that the earlier ways are the most conserving or the most cost-effective

Copyright © 1994 American Society of Agronomy, Crop Science Society of America, Soil Science Society of America, 677 S. Segoe Rd., Madison, WI 53711, USA. *Agricultural Ethics: Issues for the 21st Century*, ASA Special Publication no. 57.

ways to proceed, they may not follow these ways for tradition's sake. They might stand ready to adapt these ways to changes and opportunities in technology, cultivars, and techniques. Still, whatever their reasons, traditionalists do seek to continue familiar uses of the same resources and to ensure that agricultural practioners to come will do the same.

By contrast, industrialized agriculture is an occupation — an investment of capital — serving as means to ends that the practioner defines and understands independently of the practice of agriculture, ends such as being a family member, parent, profit seeker, and so on. These agriculturalists *are* family members who just *happen* to farm, or profit seekers who *happen* to have their capital tied up in food and fiber production. They are not primarily concerned with continuing to use the same resources now and in the future. Rather, they are opportunists with respect to methods, strategies, and resources (including cultivars), and even with respect to spending their lives in agriculture at all (Beus et al., 1991).

This conveys some rough idea of the distinctions I have in mind. All the same, we will sharpen these distinctions if we look at traditional and industrialized agriculture from four viewpoints: (i) economics, (ii) resources, (iii) culture, and (iv) ethics.

Economics

What I am referring to as traditional agriculture has some distinctive economic features. It is labor intensive rather than capital and technology intensive, and it is part of an integrated economy. Traditional agriculture is not designed to use machines, chemicals, or other technological developments for maximum yield with minimum hours of field labor. Instead, it values owner-operator cultivation of crops. In traditional agriculture, the cultivation of food and fiber is itself the only worthwhile task for which time is sought. (This is not to say, however, that traditional agriculturalists seek out drudgery nor is it to attribute a practical rigidity to traditionalists). By contrast, industrialized agriculture sees the replacement of human labor as a worthy goal because it frees the operator to perform other profitable tasks. Thus, for traditionalists, new technologies and practices must be proved as parts of a continuing way of life (MacIntyre, 1984). For the industrialist, new technologies or techniques must pass muster only as efficient and effective ways of production, independent and perhaps even incompatible with the larger set of cultural and environmental concerns. It is this difference that allows industrialized agriculture to focus solely on economic gain and high yields.

There are many possible reasons for these economic differences. The traditional agriculturalist might lack the capital to invest in technology or might see human intervention as necessary to ensure proper quality control — especially since many traditional operations are organic or rely on limited chemical inputs (e.g., Lockeretz, 1991). Traditionalists will depend on additional labor (rather than labor-saving and yield-increasing technology) as the most reliable means of cost containment. Finally, traditional agriculture often uses cooperative and familial labor for peak periods of production. This is natural because labor is a normal part of the cycle of agricultural life, not an economic commodity or input.

On the one hand, traditional agriculture is part of an economy in which the functions of producing, processing, and marketing can still be in the hands of single individuals. Wendell Berry calls these generalists "nurturers" (Berry, 1977). On the other hand, industrial agriculture creates experts in various aspects of producing, processing, marketing, and distributing food and fiber. Specialization then creates sources of income for individuals as well as corporations.

Resources

Along with mechanization and monocropping, fertilizers, pesticides, and standardized cultivars have marked the evolution of small subsistence family farms to large, industrialized, subsidized businesses serving vertically integrated companies or foreign markets. Cheap food policies, government support of international competition, subsidies favoring certain crops, publicly funded research, and agencies to assist with production have all contributed to this evolution.

Traditional agriculture, typically the agriculture of the poor, has been oriented toward subsistence and local markets. This explains why traditional farms are more diverse, more organic, and more labor intensive than industrialized agriculture units. Strategies such as intercropping, complex crop rotations, and hand weeding to control pests and to enhance fertility are common. Of course, not all traditional farms are organic. Still, the economically marginal situation of most forces them to be limited and cautious in their use of chemicals and new cultivars (e.g., Wilken, 1987; Kraybill, 1989; Hostetler, 1993). In general, the traditional agriculturalists are adaptive and coevolutionary, while industrialized agriculturalists are adoptive and standardizing.

Most traditional agriculturalists will not be early users of new technology, cultivars, or strategies because of the relatively poor financial situations of these farmers (e.g., Hayami and Ruttan, 1984). But this is not the point. Traditionalists prize their established technology, cultivars, and strategies because they have been proven, with respect to yield, sustainability of the resource, and the producers' traditional ways.

Because they preserve life and culture, traditionalists have incorporated these old ways into the rituals, economics, knowledge, and understanding of their agricultural life. Unlike the industrialists, traditionalists seem ready to define good agriculture as certain practices proven productive for certain products in local environments. Being a good farmer and enjoying the social status as one will then depend on producing the right goods, in the right (traditional) ways, in harmony with recognized cycles, limitations, and opportunities presented by the local environment. It is a matter of adapting to the environment in culturally approved ways, not a matter of adopting a practice that is the most lucrative or produces the greatest yield.

Incorporating the ideas of certain practices, crops, and technologies into the understanding of good agriculture yields a conservatism well suited to preserving food supplies and practices. Food and security are crucial to people living on the margins. To these people, the environment provides no opportunities for exploitation, only constraining limits to respect through traditional practices.

Culture

Traditional and industrialized agriculture differ in their views of the world. Let me explain. Research leading to the development of new crops and techniques for industrialized agriculture has been carried out through public funding to land grant or other universities, by private firms, or by non-governmental international consortia. The results of lab and field research have to be applicable to a wide variety of agronomic conditions. Innovations have to be coupled, therefore, with standardizing techniques to transfer to success on the farm (e.g., Altieri, 1987). This approach to agricultural production puts research and development in the hands of experts, thereby making information a commodity that is separate from farming and subsequently figures as a separate cost. This information is dependent on legal patents and copyrights, and it is controlled largely by nonproducers. Thus, within industrialized agriculture, knowledge is an institutionally isolated possession, a commodity that is shaped, controlled, and distributed by the policies and programs of government assistance, education, and commerce.

Traditional agriculture takes a holistic view of food and fiber production, one including the land, cultivars, and even the farmer's larger culture (e.g., Altieri, 1987; Wilken, 1987). Viewed holistically, the world is a web of interrelated cycles, with each one mutually adapted through coevolution. Changes in this world emerge out of the workings of the whole system, rather than as the result of certain combinations of discrete and exchangeable parts. Indeed, the whole has no parts that can be synthesized, replaced, or otherwise separated from other parts. Cultivars, soil amendments, and pest controls are all considered parts of a whole. The parts are defined in terms of their relations to each other and to the practices and larger cultural life of the farmers (Callicott, 1990).

The challenge to understanding the secrets of successful production from such a perspective is to see the various parts of the whole in relation to each other and to appreciate the nature and functioning of these patterns of relations. Some of these relationships are preserved in traditional recipes for intercropping. Others, such as planting times, are embedded symbolically in elaborate rituals, festivals, and myths of the culture and producers.

As a result, it is misleading to speak of the practice of traditional agriculture as *applying farming knowledge* to a particular field. The knowledge that transfers from field to field involves only a partial picture of that field's potential with certain types of cultivars and types of farming. We should say that traditional agriculturalists work by making their rules of thumb functional through strategies that are site-specific and imitative, or analogical. Not surprisingly, such expertise is gained from first-hand experience and personal instruction. It is not private knowledge nor is it public information, but rather a part of the traditional, daily living practices of the people. Technique is neither entirely divorced from ethos nor from cultural and moral expectations.

Ethics

The ethical goals of industrialized agriculture are often treated as abstract and independent goods to be achieved through the production of food and fiber. This fits naturally with the atomistic and reductionist world view or culture of industrialized agriculture. With such a (consequentialist) view, what is right and acceptable is what produces good consequences. Ethical concerns of traditional agriculture, such as equitable access to basic human needs, sustainability to protect future generations, and the protection of biodiversity *can be* included among these aims. All the same, these concerns are often treated as separate goods to be produced only along with maximum profit.

Such a view makes two crucial assumptions. First, that it is possible to set up a single matrix within which all good consequences are counted and treated commensurately with their proper weights. Second, that there is some way to aggregate the various goods into coherent sets to determine the best possible result from agricultural practice and policy. There are serious difficulties with each of these assumptions. Nevertheless, if these assumptions could be made good, then we could identify the best consequences in our work. We would be able then to realize the proper aim of industrialized agriculture: to amass good consequences in the greatest possible numbers.

Just how the various goods are to be typed, weighted, and aggregated is often unclear. For example, industrialized agriculturalists might assign different absolute weights or priorities to goods of different sorts, favoring those of human well-being over those of ecological integrity and nonhuman welfare (e. g., Aiken, 1984). Nevertheless, within goods of a certain sort, or for that matter within goods of a certain weight, specific instances of good (or bad) consequences may substitute one for another. This is illustrated by Luther Tweeten's utilitarian consequentialism, in which he calls for food for people and profit, without caring who eats or who profits, as long as the outcome is an optimal one of maximum profit compatible with some equitable distribution of food (Tweeten, 1983).

For the traditional agriculturalist, progress is measured in terms of successfully living the traditional way of life. The greater the harmony and integration of the individuals living these traditions, the greater the progress.

Clearly, this feature is what accounts for traditional agriculture's tendency toward sustainable conservatism and protection of resources, whereas industrialized agriculture tends toward opportunistic experimentalism and exploitation of resources. Further, the traditionalist's view of progress makes evaluation not a calculation of good to be achieved, but an appreciation and holistic understanding of which policies and practices most fully realize the traditional way of life.

There are enormous differences between traditional and industrialized agriculture because of their aims: living a way of life or achieving a maximum of good consequences. They have different viewpoints on what exists, how we know it, and how we evaluate it. In light of these differences, it is no surprise that the comparisons between traditional and industrialized agriculture are contentious and unsatisfactory. What we need is some common viewpoint from which to understand and assess each.

Goals of Traditional and Industrialized Agricultures

I believe that there should be three basic goals of any agriculture: (i) *personal* sustenance, (ii) *cultural* sustenance, and (iii) *moral* sustenance. To illustrate: through the distribution of food, industrialized agriculture has served the personal sustenance of people in Somalia by providing employment and profit for a few, as well as subsistence for some. At the same time, food assistance has taken people off the land and brought them to town or urban relief centers, while their cultural heritage of farming has been abandoned. Here, food aid has not served cultural sustenance. Furthermore, moral sustenance has not been served either, because without international policing, the distribution of food has corrupted many Somalians, reinforcing the roles of thief, gunman, and others that are not morally acceptable.

My contention is that regardless of the viewpoints of an agriculture (economics, resources, culture, and ethics), these viewpoints will be acceptable only if they effectively serve the goals of personal, cultural, *and* moral sustenance (Blatz, 1989). Most people would grant that agriculture should measure up to the task of sustainably serving at least personal sustenance and perhaps even moral sustenance (Duckham and Masefield, 1969). Many would not agree that it also should serve cultural sustenance. Cultural sustenance, however, seems to be a goal of every agricultural ethic. Personal and moral sustenance are always lived in a context of some particular cultural form. To serve personal and moral sustenance, therefore, will involve serving cultural sustenance to some degree (Kymlicka, 1989). For example, we might well wonder how it can be a triumph of industrialized agriculture to temporarily feed the people of Somalia if, in the bargain, their traditional agriculture is traded for a culture of dependence on relief agencies, and the Somalians are no longer moral agents responsible for their own subsistence.

Assessment of Traditional Agriculture

Personal sustenance of traditional agriculture can be assessed in two ways: for subsistence or for profit. In terms of subsistence, traditional agriculture *has been* reasonably successful. At the same time, traditional agriculture has been unsuccessful as a means to sustain profit.

The review is also mixed if we look at the record of traditional agriculture with respect to cultural and moral sustenance. It seems indisputable that in most cases, traditional agricultures have been the occupational staple of most culturally enduring societies. The Amish, the Appalachian hill farmers, and the Dogon of Africa are examples of this phenomenon. At the same time, however, these cultural successes have carried with them severe prices in moral sustenance. In traditional agricultures, there was often not enough food for all to eat when the available resources were reduced because population increased, climatic conditions changed, and political or economic changes threatened the society. Thus, in America, traditionalists have found themselves forced to depart from the morally approved path of small, diversified family farms serving local community markets or else to lose out economically to large, industrialized farms. Among the Amish, high land prices and the large number of children reaching adulthood within the religion conspire to drive them from their sacred calling on the land to nonagricultural employment. Here, cultural sustenance remains *somewhat* intact while moral sustenance is not fully served.

To avoid these results in personal, cultural, *and* moral sustenance, traditional agriculturalists must change. They must set aside some of their conservatism and embrace a world in process, where the processes are evolving in directions selected by traditions *and* deliberate experiments. They must be ready to leave behind the imitation of natural processes for human intervention, while at the same time maintaining concerns for sustainability and full realization of ethical autonomy for all participants (Jantsch, 1980; Emmet, 1992). Then they must replace knowing how to farm through a holistic appreciation of the world, interpreted through their fixed traditions, with an understanding growing out of their localized, evolving, and socially experimental interpretations of proper farming practices. Only in this way will they be resilient enough to meet challenges in such areas as overpopulation, resource depletion, and climate change.

Assessment of Industrialized Agriculture

Industrialized agriculture also receives mixed reviews on its ability to serve personal, cultural, and moral sustenance. Industrialized agriculture should turn more in the direction of traditional agriculture. In terms of short-term service to personal sustenance for profit, industrialized agriculture is greatly superior to traditional. Equally without dispute is the superior record of industrialized agriculture with respect to short-term subsistence needs.

Although traditional agriculture has fed a larger percentage of the world's people for a greater period of time, industrialized agriculture feeds enormous numbers for little effort, and it promises to feed more of the world's people in the future with less labor. But the good news is not, as touted in the USA, that we will have more food with less labor. There is a long and distinguished tradition in which work in general, and agricultural work in particular, is culturally and morally important to human living (Montmarquet, 1989). Rather, industrialized agriculture has given us a way to absorb subsistence (and possibly even profit) losses due to diminishing agricultural resources resulting from urbanization, population increases, and environmental degradation. Still, there is no dispute that industrialized agriculture brings with it great problems of resource degradation; the question remains — can our industrialized strategies prove sustainable? (Cronon, 1983; Merchant, 1989). The answer is that this agriculture does not seem to be sustainable (Davis, 1992; Jackson, 1980; Odum and Franz, 1980).

Although classical industrialized agriculture's record of *sustainable* service to personal sustenance seems mixed at best, not even this much can be said with respect to cultural and moral sustenance. The consolidation of proprietorship has limited the ability of people to live in a culture of small, diversified family farms and rural community life. With this has gone much of their moral accountability for resource and cultivar conservation. Just as some Amish farmers (who now work in small manufacturing firms) have lost touch with their resource, the land, other farmers, who lose their way of life when taken off their land, also face a situation in which they have no moral or cultural accountability for conservation. For other former agriculturalists, industrialization has made things even worse in terms of moral and cultural sustenance. Woes of unemployment are compounded by well-known urban troubles as cities become places where it is difficult to live a life of full moral agency with accountability for the natural and social environments. This is the plight, for example, of many African-Americans who migrated to northern cities with the mechanization of cotton farming (Lemann, 1991).

Remedies for industrialized agriculture's failure to ensure personal, moral, and cultural sustenance may take food and fiber production back toward a greater labor intensiveness and smaller scale farms. But at the same time, we can move forward in our thinking about problems of production, not so much through a traditionalist's holistic appreciation of particular practices or policies, as through the traditionalist's understanding of ecological processes. From this new viewpoint we will recognize that some substitutions within the parts of production are possible, that some standardizations are useful and sustainable, and that some aspects of production can be understood abstractly in their general outlines. The difference will be that this work will have the traditionalist's respect for ecological processes and will have a readiness to adapt production experiments to site-specific requirements. Industrialized agriculture seems better able to meet all the ethically important concerns of personal, cultural, and moral sustenance *if* it sets aside its world of totally independent parts, its way of knowing the world by generally abstracted analysis, and its sole value of resource-exploiting accumulation.

Coming Full Circle

I began by asking how agriculture can feed the world today and maintain sustainability for tomorrow. I suggested that the viewpoints of traditional and industrialized agricultures adjust accordingly, so that both forms of producing food and fiber can be brought closer together, each united with the other under a new set of goals. All agricultural endeavors will be local adaptations of these new common goals and reflect the experimentalism of industrialized agriculture and something like the ecological respect (Blatz, 1991b) and conservatism of traditional agriculture. Just what these new common goals should be will depend on the specific challenges we confront as we pursue the goals of personal, cultural, and moral sustenance through agriculture in a crowded and environmentally abused world.

References

Aiken, W. 1984. Ethical issues in agriculture. p. 247–288. *In* T. Regan (ed.) Earthbound: New introductory essays in environmental ethics. Random House, New York.

Altieri, M.A. 1987. Agroecology: The scientific basis of alternative agriculture. Westview Press, Boulder, CO.

Avery, D. 1985. U.S. farm dilemma: The global bad news is wrong. Science (Washington, DC) 230:408–412.

Berry, W. 1977. The unsettling of America: Culture and agriculture. Sierra Club Books, San Francisco.

Beus, C.E., R.E. Dunlap, R.M. Jimmerson, and W.L. Holmes. 1991. Competing paradigms: The debate bewteen alternative and conventional agriculture. Res. Bull. XB1020. Washington State Univ., Pullman.

Blatz, C.V. 1989. Contextualism and critical thinking: Programmatic investigations. Educ. Theory 39:107–119.

Blatz, C.V. 1991a. Ethics and agriculture. An anthology on current issues in world context. Univ. of Idaho Press, Moscow.

Blatz, C.V. 1991b. It is morally permissable to manipulate the genome of domestic hogs. J. Agric. Environ. Ethics 4:166–176.

Blatz, C. 1992. The very idea of sustainability. Agric. Human Values 9:12–28.

Callicott, J.B. 1990. The metaphysical transition in farming: From the Newtonian–mechanical to the Eltonian ecological. J. Agric. Ethics 3:36–49.

Cronon, W. 1983. Changes in the land: Indians, colonists, and the ecology of New England. Hill and Wang, New York.

Davis, T. 1992. Arizona's water disaster: A $4 billion project provides water, but few can afford to buy it. High Country News 24:10-14.

Duckham, A.N., and G.B. Masefield. 1969. Farming systems of the world. Praeger Publ., New York.

Duvick, D.N. 1991. Genetic diversity and plant breeding. p. 492–298. *In* C.V. Blatz (ed.) Ethics and agriculture. An anthology on current issues in world context. Univ. of Idaho Press, Moscow.

Easterbrook, G. 1985. Making sense of agriculture. Atlantic Monthly 256:63–78.

Emmet, D. 1992. The passage of nature. Temple Univ. Press, Philadelphia.

Hayami, Y., and V. Ruttan. 1984. The green revolution: Inducement and distribution. Pak. Dev. Rev. 23:37–63.

Hostetler, J.A. 1993. Amish society. 4th ed. Johns Hopkins Univ. Press, Baltimore.

Jackson, W. 1980. New roots for agriculture. Univ. of Nebraska Press, Lincoln.

Jantsch, E. 1980. The self-organizing universe: Scientific and human implications of the emerging paradigm of evolution. Pergamon Press, Oxford, England.

Kraybill, D.B. 1989. The riddle of Amish culture. Johns Hopkins Univ. Press, Baltimore.

Kymlicka, W. 1989. Liberalism, community, and culture. Clarendon Press, Oxford, England.

Lemann, N. 1991. The promised land: The great Black migration and how it changed America. Alfred A. Knopf, New York.

Lockeretz, W. 1991. Information requirements of reduced-chemical production methods. Am. J. Altern. Agric. 6:97–103.

MacIntyre, A.C. 1984. After virtue: A study in moral theory. 2nd ed. Univ. of Notre Dame Press, Notre Dame, IN.

Merchant, C. 1989. Ecological revolutions: Nature, gender, and science in New England. Univ. of North Carolina Press, Chapel Hill.

Montmarquet, J.A. 1989. The idea of agrarianism: From hunter-gatherer to agrarian radical in Western culture. Univ. of Idaho Press, Moscow.

Odum, E.P., and E.H. Franz. 1980. Whither the life support system? p. 263–274. In N. Polunin (ed.) Growth without ecodisasters? Halsted-Wiley, New York.

Strange, M. 1988. Family farming: A new economic vision. Univ. of Nebraska Press, Lincoln.

Tweeten, L. 1983. Food for people and profit: Ethics and capitalism. p. 1–8. In Farm and food system in transition series, no. 5. Michigan State Univ. Coop. Ext. Serv., East Lansing.

Wilken, G.C. 1987. Good farmers: Traditional agricultural resource management in Mexico and Central America. Univ. of California Press, Berkeley.

6   What Is Good Agriculture?

C. Dean Freudenberger

Luther Seminary
St. Paul, Minnesota

In order to address the subject of agricultural ethics and how ethical perceptions help to identify issues for the 21st century, I raise the question, "What
is good agriculture?" This question confronts us within the contexts of both
environmental threat and the growing consumption of nonrenewable resources.
During the past 20 years, a great deal of work has been done in the fields of
medical, business, legal, and environmental ethics, but to my knowledge, a
book has yet to be entitled *Agricultural Ethics*. My colleague at this symposium, Charles V. Blatz, has edited a first-of-its-kind anthology entitled
Ethics and Agriculture (1991). For several years, Richard P. Haynes has edited
the fine journal *Agriculture and Human Values*. In the first issue of this
journal, H.O. Kunkel (1984), stated:

> The problem for the agricultural establishment and other interested parties is that
> there has been little adequate normative scholarship to provide knowledge of
> goodness and badness or about situations and consequences for handling the
> increasing numbers of problems coming out of technological advances in
> agriculture, institutional change and societal metamorphosis.

Kunkel's essay then pointed to the need for work in the field of agricultural
ethics. Slowly and surely we are moving toward the time when we can
consider some major works that dare to pioneer in this area. At this time, the
most common response to "What is good agriculture?" is "Maximized
yields." Of course, there is much more to be considered. What follows is
another effort to explore this long overlooked and short-changed question.

As we approach the next century we are asking, as a global human
community, "What's for dinner?" The next question comes quickly, "Will
there be food for tomorrow?" The importance of agriculture can be seen in
these basic questions. Is there any subject more critical? No society in recorded
history has circumvented the questions about a reliable food supply for very
long. If the political, economic, and social orders give less than priority
attention to these basic questions, then it is not long before the realities of soil
and water loss and the migration of a destitute rural people to the cities result
in a collapsed domestic food system. When this happens, it is usually too late
for restoration. To understand this, every first-year student in the agricultural
sciences (as well as in the social sciences and history) ought to read: *The*

Copyright © 1994 American Society of Agronomy, Crop Science Society of America, Soil Science
Society of America, 677 S. Segoe Rd., Madison, WI 53711, USA. *Agricultural Ethics: Issues for
the 21st Century*, ASA Special Publication no. 57.

Conquest of the Land through 7,000 Years (Lowdermilk, 1975), and *Desertification: Its Causes and Consequences* (Secretariat of the United Nations Conference on Desertification, 1977).

The Point of Departure into the Subject of Agricultural Ethics

As we ponder the food prospects of future generations, we frequently ask, "Why care about the future in the first place?" The reply, "I could care less!" shows the attitude of our culture. Here it is important to suggest that caring about any person or thing, nonhuman life, soil, water, air, food for tomorrow, the shape and future of our professional fields of endeavor, is our only tangible way of expressing gratitude for life and our opportunity to participate in it. Finding ways to say "thanks" is what makes us human. Choosing to care is an act of responsible freedom. This freedom to choose to be responsible, or to care about the future, ought to be understood as a basic human right. If, for whatever reason, we are unable to choose freely to care, we are denied a fundamental element of our humanity. Basic to our thinking about agricultural ethics and the ethical issues rising on the horizon is the need to clarify the issue of caring. Why care for the future? Why work hard in our professional fields to assure the welfare of future generations whom we will never know? Why work hard to design an agriculture that meets the needs of the present without compromising the ability of future generations to meet their needs (World Commission on Environment and Development, 1987)? Again, we ought to care because we have a basic human need to acknowledge the wondrous miracle of life. The motivation of gratitude is high on the scale of moral maturation (Kohlberg, 1981, 1984) and is the essence of ethical decision making. This leads us beyond primitive ethical foundations of rewards and punishments or enlightened self-interest.

A Personal History of Reflection about Good Agriculture

For me, the question about good agriculture emerges from a long personal history of worldwide involvement with the subject of agricultural development. During my 40-year career, the focus of my work was to overcome the legacies of domestic food shortages as a result of the long emphasis of European colonial export cropping. Prior to the 1960s, research and development in agriculture focused on the production of crops such as tea, coffee, cocoa, sugar cane, cotton, livestock, pineapple, rubber, pyrethrum, coconut, and bananas. The principle commitment to agriculture in this period was production for export by the colonial powers. The welfare of indigenous peoples, their cultures, patterns of land tenure, and conservation of traditional grassland and forest resources was not in the colonial development formula. From the 1950s through the 1970s, (and in many places even to this day), agricultural development involved, by and large, technical transfers from temperate to tropical zones. In most situations, these technologies and their purposes were dysfunctional in different ecosystems and human cultures. I have observed the breakdown, to the point of collapse, of agricultural infrastructures — from rural banks and markets to roads, bridges, storage and food processing facilities, rural health services, and responsible public police security. The result is that today (with predictable increases in human populations during the next century) there are more than 40 food-deficit nations, plus soil, forest, and grassland degradation almost beyond comprehension. We are aware of the dimensions and complexities of hunger and poverty, along with soil loss, deforestation, and species extinction.

There is one thing that I have learned for certain during my life: rural community welfare, environmental health (including the preservation of basic agricultural resources such as water, soil, species, grasslands, and forests), and agricultural science, technology, and industry are inextricably bound together when the questions are asked, "What's for dinner?" and "Will there be food for tomorrow?" We can no longer proceed with the development of agriculture in an isolated fashion involving specialized disciplines. All three components of the agricultural question (rural community welfare, the environment, and agricultural science, technology, and industry) must be addressed in ways that consider simultaneously the needs of each part of the equation.

I have learned also of the need for historical knowledge about our agriculture. Midway through my career I recognized the necessity to examine basic assumptions about any given agricultural system and to think about what ought to be, rather than what is, and how to keep the existing system working a little longer. At this point I would like to suggest that the most practical thing we can do today is to work with the question about what ought to be; otherwise, we simply add momentum to the pace of human as well as natural resource exhaustion. I believe that this need for normative reflection is what elicited Kunkel's statement at the beginning of this essay.

It was during my work with the U.S. Peace Corps in Sahelian West Africa that I developed six questions which provided the working basis for various projects. Although these questions evolved during my work in West Africa, they also applied to other continents. I believe that these questions are relevant to the serious issues in U.S. agriculture for the years ahead.

1. What did the original ecosystem look like before industrialized agriculture?
2. How did indigenous people interrelate to each ecosystem before industrialized agriculture?
3. What do these ecosystems look like today or to what degree have these complex ecosystems been simplified?
4. How did this transformation take place or what were the engines of this change?
5. What might be the design of a new agriculture that mimics or functions as a close analogue to the system before industrialized agriculture?

6. What is the new design for agricultural development that moves us toward this analogue?

As we shall see, these questions can provide us with a way to think about "What is good agriculture?"

The following quotation from *Only One Earth* (Ward and Dubos, 1972), the study document for the delegates of the 1972 United Nations Conference on the Human Environment in Stockholm, articulates our contemporary challenge with a unique historical perspective, and these words have influenced my thinking ever since. They preceded the United Nations Conference on Environment and Development in Rio de Janeiro by 20 years! They come at the end of Chapter 1, appropriately entitled, "The World We Inherit":

> In short, the two worlds of man [sic] ... the biosphere of his inheritance, the technosphere of his creation ... are out of balance, indeed potentially in deep conflict. And man is in the middle. This is the hinge of history at which we stand, the door of the future opening on to a crisis more sudden, more global, more inescapable, and more bewildering than any ever encountered by the human species and one which will take decisive shape within the life span of children who are already born.

Indeed, the biosphere of our inheritance and the technosphere of our creation are in deep conflict. This is unique. It is historically unprecedented. We are professionals serving the associated fields of the science of agronomy, standing before a doorway opening onto a situation unprecedented in human history.

If there is to be a future, then this conflict of history must be resolved, and soon. Conflict resolution in our agricultural sciences and technology, if it is to happen, as it must, will involve a revolutionary shift from extractive to regenerative technology in three dimensions: human community, environment, and science, technology, and industry. We must develop an agriculture that can approximate the dynamics of the bioregional ecosystems in which it unfolds. This is a massive challenge. At this time, there are but a few clues. Yet if we work hard, perhaps we can begin to realize this type of an agriculture within the next half-century. This is the most fundamental challenge facing 21st-century agriculture: it must become solar and biologically based instead of petrochemically based. We cannot go on much longer with our high dependencies of farm inputs based on nonrenewable resources, from P to oil (Gever et al., 1991). Biotic communities cannot sustain much longer the impact of the moldboard plow associated with monocultures, petrochemicals, and the demise of the farming communities and their cultures. This is the type of forceful conclusions one makes after 40 years of global observation of the attempts of societies to provide enough food for dinner today and tomorrow. The USA is not exempt from this observation. What we see today is a further reinforcement of Lowdermilk's (1975) conclusion about the loss of vegetative cover and soil erosion during 7000 years of land conquest.

Needed Historical Perspective for Agricultural Ethics

Historical analysis will be an essential element of agricultural ethics issues in the future. If there is to be something for dinner, we must break free from the assumptions of contemporary agriculture, whether it is here in the USA or in Sahelian Africa, the coconut-covered islands of the Pacific, or the rubber plantations of Southeast Asia. For gaining a fresh perspective on U.S. agriculture, I found two works of value: *A Forest Journey: The Role of Wood in the Development of Civilization* (Perlin, 1989), and *Changes in the Land: Indians, Colonists and the Ecology of New England* (Cronon, 1983). In these histories, one catches a glimpse of the productivity of earlier times and the way that people related to the landscape. These books help to clarify the first two of the six questions that I raised.

These works complement Kirschenmann's (1993) essay on rediscovering American agriculture. He focuses on the question, "What has happened to U.S. agriculture since the arrival of Columbus in 1492?" He suggests that nothing really happened in U.S. agriculture until the Europeans arrived and the plow unzipped the prairie. Until that time, impressive numbers of people had practiced a sophisticated agriculture for thousands of years. It was an agriculture that reflected the accumulated wisdom of the past generations. It was an agriculture that fit the landscape. It was an agriculture of restraint — the opposite of the extractive agriculture introduced by Europeans.

As the fertility of the soil gave out, extraction in the form of minerals to maintain the soil fertility became the new norm. First, the organic nutrient fraction was exhausted. Now inorganics maintain industrialized agriculture a little longer. The practices of the previous agriculture of restraint, utilizing technologies of recycling, moisture conservation, bioregional plant selectivity, and plant and animal diversity, were substituted with new minerals from outside the system. Mining essential resources has worked well for the past 150 years, if the full costs to people and their culture, soil loss, soil fertility, oil, gas, toxic wastes, and the centralization of production and markets are not measured. Modern mechanization and the inputs of fertilizers and pesticides have replaced farmers and their communities. Wealth generated by this system now goes out of the community and largely into the hands of distant food processors and suppliers of capital and materials. A crop surplus from this marvel of high technology has become a further problem affecting the international community of nations.

Kirschenmann (1993) asks, "After the depletion of human and natural resources, then what? Will there be food for tomorrow?" Kirschenmann identifies three options. First, we can stay on the present course. But for how much longer can this direction be followed? Second, we can work for a technological fix by making adjustments to the problems that are now so apparent. With this option, however, there are questions about who will benefit (Busch et al., 1991). Our track record of prediction about such matters, particularly over the long run, is not impressive. Our third option is regenerative food systems. This option takes a whole-systems approach. It works toward analogues of the original bioregional landscape. The regenerative option assumes a caring culture — a culture that is in part governed by the value of healthy prospects for future generations and a healthy landscape. For example, people at The Land Institute near Salina, KS, are working toward a substitute for wheat and barley with the development of indigenous prairie grasses in perennial polycultures (Jackson, 1985; Soule and Piper, 1992). This research also moves toward the development of what Kirschenmann calls an "agriculture of restraint." It points to the possibilities on the other side of the industrial extractive agricultural model that has evolved since the time of Columbus.

Toward Normative Thinking about Agriculture

During the 1960s I encountered the works of Aldo Leopold. He wrote about the importance and function of a land ethic (1966):

> ... a land ethic changes the role of *Homo sapiens* from conqueror of the land-community to plain member and citizen of it. It implies respect for his [sic] fellow-members, and also respect for the community as such.

I found myself repeatedly asking the question, "What is good agriculture?" Leopold's land ethic provided me with a clear summary of all the works in social and environmental ethics:

> A thing is right when it tends to preserve the integrity, stability, and beauty of the biotic community. It is wrong when it tends otherwise.

Meine's (1988) biography of Leopold aptly delineates the years of experience that are reflected in Leopold's ethic. His ethical insight emerged out of travels and reflections during the early years of this century. It is as profoundly challenging as it is simple. Its implications for the research and development of a post-industrial agriculture are enormous. Serious thinking about this ethical proposition challenges us to search for a way to make a transition from the reductionism in our extractive agriculture to one that mimics the complexities of natural systems. In this we might find stability over the long run, or a perspective of time that is needed to replace the mode of our historical period, namely, short-run success.

A Normative Definition

A responsible agriculture can be defined as an agriculture that ultimately enhances the health and maintains the integrity and stability of the natural system with which it interacts. If we take the challenge of planetary survival as a determining principle in how we think and act, then this definition about good agriculture might be evaluated as having merit. It is out of a sense of gratitude for life and our moment in it (reflecting some meaning into the ethical idea of responsible freedom) that this type of working definition emerges. Enhancement is a powerful term. Furthermore, the idea of enhancement gives us a sense of goal. Without goals we are unable to focus our research or to identify the most important issues in agriculture that must be resolved. The absence of clear goals, such as enhancement of the landscape and the rural community, makes public understanding of and commitment to new agricultural futures very difficult. If we are to avoid future problems, policy makers, business, and industry must do essential planning now.

Guidelines for Normative Work

I would like to suggest the following guidelines for an *enhanced agriculture*: (i) species are preserved (instead of extirpated), (ii) health and fertility of the land are strengthened from generation to generation (the soil is rebuilt and its organic matter increased), (iii) ecological integrity and justice in personal and community relationships are enhanced, and (iv) agricultural technologies for the production of food and fiber are self-reliant and regenerative from generation to generation.

The goals of an enhanced agriculture involve (i) improving ecological integrity by increasing the symbiotic relationships of land, agriculture, and society, (ii) contributing to the health of the whole community of life, and (iii) caring for the earth. We ought to understand this third goal from the perspective of "the conflict of the technosphere of our creation and the biosphere of our inheritance" (Ward and Dubos, 1972).

The national, bioregional, and local biotic community strategy that we might follow for the creation of an enhanced agriculture will require research into agroecology (Altieri, 1987; Gliessman, 1990). This approach also involves rehabilitating and enhancing rural communities, preserving prime agricultural lands by public policy and legislation, and creating production and pricing mechanisms that ensure fairness and financial stability for the primary producer. It becomes clear that the agricultural challenge is a massive one for all sectors of society.

Toward a New Concept of Agricultural Efficiency

As one struggles with the implications of the land ethic of Leopold and incorporates its normative conceptualizations into the field of agriculture, the concept of agricultural efficiency can be broadened in more ways than maximum yield. Is it possible to think about efficiency in terms of progress in domestic self-reliance on a regenerative basis (i.e., enhanced relationships between the land, society, and agriculture)? Agricultural efficiency needs to be defined in ways that address the ability of each nation, from generation to generation, to feed its people. We must ask, "Is the measure of efficiency in agricultural production consistent and coherent with the dream of a world without hunger?" It is necessary to remind ourselves that consistency and coherency between means and ends relationships are also critical elements in moral behavior.

Value Foundations and Normative Thought

Ethical formulations rest on value propositions. It seems to me that the values for agriculture for the next century are: (i) health of the land, (ii) welfare of future generations, (iii) social and interspecies justice, and (iv) integrity in meaningful work and relationships (Freudenberger, 1986). Finally, a fifth value in the idea of an enhanced agriculture is the value of caring. This value (usually overlooked) was suggested in the beginning of this essay as basic to the design of good agriculture. Values are inseparable from an agricultural ethic. Agriculture is a complex subject that cannot be addressed effectively with narrow disciplinary approaches. If the three inextricable components of agriculture (community, environment, and the sciences, technologies, and industries of agriculture) do not interact symbiotically, eventually things fall apart. This is the lesson in the history of land conquest over 7000 years.

Four Categories of Agricultural Issues

The first category of agricultural issues is the conversion to a post-petroleum food system. The World Commission on Environment and Development (1987) reminds us of the precarious nature of our present world food supply. It is frightenly dependent on inputs of N derived from rapidly depleting nonrenewable resources. The successes of the Green Revolution give us a little more time to feed ourselves while we begin the research and development of a solar and biologically intensive technology (an agroecology) — the building of an agriculture beyond "extraction." We must continue to ask, "What are the prospects of the next generations to feed themselves if we continue, right up to the point of resource exhaustion, our petrochemically based food technologies? Do we have the commitment for the long and arduous research task for an alternative agriculture?" (National Research Council, 1989). These are intensely moral questions.

The second category of issues is the resolution of the growing stress placed on the rural community and large numbers of farmers and farm families (Comstock, 1987). We cannot dream of a post-petroleum, regenerative food system that enhances the land and community from generation to generation, without vibrant and economically secure rural people and the continual entry of young farmers into agriculture (Strange, 1988). Berry (1977) observed that we have pondered this issue since Thomas Jefferson. As we sow, so shall we reap. If we sow centralization in our domestic food system, so shall we reap the consequences (Goldschmidt, 1947). Centralization of any human endeavor, whether it be political, industrial, or both, excludes the necessary participation of would-be innovators, including youth. This exclusion ultimately lowers the abilities of communities, as well as the whole food system, to change when the recognition of the need for change becomes clear (Kuhn, 1962).

The third category of issues concerns quality, production, processing, and distribution of healthy and safe food. This involves not only our cropping systems but also how we are producing livestock. The issues of large confinement livestock operations, genetic alterations, and the impact of these systems on human health, the health of the environment and rural farming communities, and the prospects of once again developing diversified and integrated farming systems have to be confronted (Mason and Singer, 1990). Solutions need to be found to the growing risk factors of human and environmental health over the *long run*. We ought to proceed with great caution because spinoffs (many barely predicted at this time) can be negative, too.

The fourth category of issues concerns international commodity surplus and trade. The present worldwide surplus of agricultural commodities has been in the making for the past 50 years. It will take that long to make a smooth transition to new structures and systems. How do we even begin to think through the required adjustments in agricultural production and international trade? Comparative trade advantage must be rethought if we are to talk about regenerative and self-reliant global food systems. At this moment in our modern industrialized world, it takes an enormous amount of oil to move commodities from one side of the globe to another, whether by truck, train, ship, or aircraft. As we think about international commodity trade, we assume that the structures of colonial agriculture, firmly established during the past century and a half, will continue to prevail. The question has to shift from "How shall we feed the world?" to "How can the nations of the world become sustainably self-reliant in their food supplies now that we are beyond the colonial period?" Can the dream of a world without hunger become a reality in the next century? If so, what are the implications for change that this dream implies? Closely associated with this category of issues is population growth. As complex as this is, a fundamental observation is clear: poverty, as a symptom of injustice, is the breeding ground for rapid population growth (World Commission on Environment and Development, 1987).

Summary

I am certain that for many of my colleagues, reading this essay has been difficult. Working within the reductionist paradigm that up until now has served us so well makes it difficult to shift comfortably to a whole-systems approach. My work began with the reductionist model firmly in place. It took me a quarter of a century, mostly beyond the borders of my home culture, to make a transition to a model that is quite different. I did not move easily from one to the other. Rather, global encounters with the legacies of our modern era pushed me reluctantly into recognizing the importance of looking at agriculture from a different perspective. It was a painful experience but I am grateful for it. My assumptions were shattered.

The need for normative thinking has been suggested in this and other essays of the symposium. I have tried to show the connections between values and normative conceptualizations and the function of normative thought in defining goals and issues of agriculture. I have tried to identify the need for goals. I have attempted to show that a land and community enhancing agriculture cannot orbit around a society that goes the other way. They are all tied together. If, as agriculturalists of whichever particular discipline and expertise, we pay attention to agricultural history and the history of the rise and fall of civilizations from an ecological perspective (commonly overlooked in our history books), we will be better equipped to define more clearly the agenda in agricultural research and development for the 21st century. Historical perspectives serve as a reminder of the inseparability of agricultural science and industry. These perspectives serve to help us understand the relationships between the health and stability of rural communities of primary producers and the health of the microbiotic communities in which they find themselves. History helps us see that the maintenance, health, and integrity of the natural systems, with their complex relations of interdependence, are critical to the questions ''What's for dinner?'' and ''Will there be food for tomorrow?''

We must think about our options for a different future. We might ask, ''How can tomorrow's agriculture be designed to serve the needs of the land and the caregivers of the land?'' We also need to ask about the design of national and global infrastructures that will be coherent and consistent with the normative concept about an enhanced agriculture for a self-reliant community of nations. We cannot have a ''care-full'' agriculture without a care-giving social, economic, technical and industrial infrastructure, which depends on the research community for answers. A prerequisite for change in the direction of what I have repeatedly referred to as an enhanced agriculture involves a positive response to my first question, ''Why care?'' We care because we are grateful.

References

Altieri, M.A. 1987. Agroecology: The scientific basis of alternative agriculture. Westview Press, Boulder, CO.

Berry, W. 1977. The unsettling of America: Culture & agriculture. Sierra Club Books, San Francisco.

Blatz, C.V. 1991. Ethics and agriculture: An anthology on current issues in world context. Univ. of Idaho Press, Moscow.

Busch, L., and W.B. Lacy. 1983. Science, agriculture, and the politics of research. Westview Press, Boulder, CO.

Busch, L., W.B. Lacy, J. Burkhardt, and L.R. Lacy. 1991. Plants, power, and profit: Social, economic, and ethical consequences of the new biotechnologies. Blackwell Sci. Publ., Boston.

Comstock, G. 1987. Is there a moral obligation to save the family farm? Iowa State Univ. Press, Ames.

Cronon, W. 1983. Changes in the land: Indians, colonists, and the ecology of New England. Hill and Wang, New York.

Freudenberger, C.D. 1986. Value and ethical dimensions of alternative agricultural approaches: In quest of a regenerative and just agriculture. p. 348–364. *In* K. Dahlberg (ed.) New directions for agriculture and agricultural research: Neglected dimensions and emerging alternatives. Rowman & Allanheld, Totowa, NJ.

Gever, J., R. Kaufmann, D. Skole, and C. Vörösmarty. 1991. Beyond oil: The threat to food and fuel in the coming decades. 3rd ed. Univ. Press of Colorado, Niwot.

Gliessman, S.R. (ed.). 1990. Agroecology: Researching the ecological basis for sustainable agriculture. Springer-Verlag, New York.

Goldschmidt, W. 1947. As you sow: Three studies in the social consequences of agribusiness. Free Press, Glencoe, IL.

Jackson, W. 1985. New roots for agriculture. Univ. of Nebraska Press, Lincoln.

Jacobson, J.L. 1992. Gender bias: Roadblock to sustainable development. Worldwatch Pap. 110. Worldwatch Inst., Washington, DC.

Kirschenmann, F. 1993. Rediscovering American agriculture. Word World 13:294–303.

Kohlberg, L. 1981. The philosophy of moral development: Moral stages and the idea of justice. Harper & Row, San Francisco.

Kohlberg, L. 1984. The psychology of moral development: Moral stages and the life cycle. Harper & Row, San Francisco.

Kuhn, T.S. 1962. The structure of scientific revolutions. Univ. of Chicago Press, Chicago.

Kunkel, H.O. 1984. Agriculture ethics — the setting. Agric. Human Values 1:20–23.

Leopold, A. 1966. A Sand County almanac: With other essays on conservation from Round River. Oxford Univ. Press, New York.

Lowdermilk, W.C. 1975. Conquest of the land through 7,000 years. USDA-SCS Agric. Inf. Bull. 99. U.S. Gov. Print. Office, Washington, DC.

Mason, J., and P. Singer. 1990. Animal factories. Harmony Books, New York.

Meine, C. 1988. Aldo Leopold: His life and work. Univ. of Wisconsin Press, Madison.

Nash, R. 1989. The rights of nature: A history of environmental ethics. Univ. of Wisconsin Press, Madison.

National Research Council. 1989. Alternative agriculture. Natl. Academy Press, Washington, DC.

Perlin, J. 1989. A forest journey: The role of wood in the development of civilization. W.W. Norton & Co., New York.

Secretariat of the United Nations Conference on Desertification. 1977. Desertification: Its causes and consequences. Pergamon Press, New York.

Soule, J.D., and J.K. Piper. 1992. Farming in nature's image: An ecological approach to agriculture. Island Press, Washington, DC.

Strange, M. 1988. Family farming: A new economic vision. Univ. of Nebraska Press, Lincoln.

Vogeler, I. 1981. The myth of the family farm: Agribusiness dominance of U.S. agriculture. Westview Press, Boulder, CO.

Ward, B., and R. Dubos. 1972. Only one earth: The care and maintenance of a small planet. W.W. Norton & Co., New York.

World Commission on Environment and Development. 1987. Our common future. Oxford Univ. Press, New York.

7   Teaching Agricultural Ethics

Thomas A Ruehr

California Polytechnic State University
San Luis Obispo, California

Why should we in agriculture be concerned about ethics? After all, haven't we been acting ethically? Don't we help to feed the world? Yes, but that is not enough. We need to confront a major dilemma in our contemporary society. John Steinbeck (1951) described it in *The Log from the Sea of Cortez*:

> There is a strange duality in the human which makes for an ethical paradox. We have definitions of good qualities and of bad; not changing things, but generally considered good and bad throughout the ages and throughout the species. Of the good, we think always of wisdom, tolerance, kindliness, generosity, humility; and the qualities of cruelty, greed, self-interest, graspingness, and rapacity are universally considered undesirable. And yet in our structure of society, the so-called and considered good qualities are invariable concomitants of failure, while the bad ones are the cornerstones of success. A man [sic] — a viewing-point man — while he will love the abstract good qualities and detest the abstract bad, will nevertheless envy and admire the person who through possessing the bad qualities has succeeded economically and socially, and will hold in contempt that person whose good qualities have caused failure. When such a viewing-point man thinks of Jesus or St. Augustine or Socrates he regards them with love because they are the symbols of the good he admires, and he hates the symbols of the bad. But actually he would rather be successful than good.

Thus, we often see ethics as something that is good to have but not to deal with in our daily lives. From an ethical perspective, the basic problem evolves from a conflict between short-term "success" and the long-term ultimate "good." Too often we want the former but cannot survive unless we have the latter. This duality reflects the basic underlying conflict of values that we see today.

We are faced constantly with decisions in agriculture; many are value laden, and they make us aware of conflict. Decision-making requires care, cooperation, consensus building, conflict management, and the resolution of divergent goals. Acting ethically forces people to cooperate, to move beyond themselves, and to develop a greater concern for fellow human beings, animals, and the environment. Ethics helps us understand the emotions and feelings associated with each ethical issue.

To become effective in decision-making we need to identify what values we hold and understand why we cherish them. To be effective in our global

Copyright © 1994 American Society of Agronomy, Crop Science Society of America, Soil Science Society of America, 677 S. Segoe Rd., Madison, WI 53711, USA. *Agricultural Ethics: Issues for the 21st Century*, ASA Special Publication no. 57.

environment and society we must understand why other people hold different values. Too often, we become so frustrated in trying to make a decision that we choose not to decide. This is actually a decision, however, and must be recognized as such. Philosophical debate allows us to recognize our own values. I believe this is a central tenet. *We learn ethics by arguing about what we believe and do not believe.*

Conflicting Ethical Concepts

There are several different approaches to an ethical dilemma. An example of water use illustrates that even the major philosophical and ethical tools can conflict with one another. A *utilitarian approach* says that we should use irrigation water to provide the most benefit for the most people. This would be achieved by summing individual values and preferences. For a diminishing rural population (with decreasing political clout), this means that an urban population would benefit more from using the water. A *rights-based approach* says "I don't care about that, I know that I have a right to use water just as I've always used it." Note that this approach emphasizes not only one's *legal* rights, but also assumes that one is exerting one's *moral* rights, which is not the case. An *intrinsic value* or *holistic approach* (which stresses love, reverence, compassion, aesthetics, and respect for nature) argues that regardless of one's rights or the overall utility, we must preserve the integrity of the environment for future generations. These approaches are all different and conflict with one another. We must not bury or suppress such conflict, but embrace it.

We seek to exert our *rights* at every opportunity. The intensely litigious nature of the U.S. society is fed in part by a judicial system that profits from our interests in rights (as long as "I win"). What we have lost is the concept of avoiding litigation by acting in a proper and respectful manner toward all others. The emphasis on duties, responsibilities, and obligations to others must balance our interest in exerting only our rights, because we have no rights without the associated responsibilities. We must always hold these in balance or, more properly, in tension.

Courses in Agricultural Ethics

In 1981, the U.S. Department of Agriculture's Joint Council on Food and Agricultural Sciences, through the National Higher Education Committee, identified goals for improving instruction in higher education in agriculture. One of the major areas for emphasis was ethics and public policy (Merritt, 1984; Wilson and Morren, 1990). In 1984, an interdisciplinary team was organized to develop curriculum resources in the area of ethics and public policy, such that by 1987, a national teacher training program at the University of Kentucky presented curriculum materials regarding this area of emphasis. While only a few universities had courses in agricultural ethics in 1984, since

Table 1. Alphabetical listing of universities that have offered or are currently offering courses in agricultural ethics.

University	Instructor	Department
Cal Poly State Univ.	T. Ruehr†	Soil Science
	S. Dundon	Philosophy
California State Univ. (Chico)	M. Baldy	Agriculture
Cornell University	R. Baer†	Natural Resources
Iowa State University	G. Comstock	Philosophy
Ohio State University	T. Stout	Agricultural Economics
Purdue University	J. Vorst	Agronomy
Rutgers University	R. Matthews†	Philosophy
Texas A&M University	P. Thompson†	Philosophy
	H. Kunkel†	Nutrition
University of California (Davis)	D. Jolly	Agronomy
University of Florida	J. Burkhardt†	Philosophy
University of Georgia	P. Hartel	Crop and Soil Sciences
	F. Ferré	Philosophy
University of Idaho	K. George	Philosophy
University of Maryland	M. Sagoff†	Philosophy
University of Wyoming	J. Lockwood	Entomology

† Members of the 1987 Agriculture Ethics and Public Policy team.

the training program several other universities have joined in teaching agricultural ethics (Table 1).

An Example of an Agricultural Ethics Course

I would like to use the "Human Values in Agriculture" course at my university, Cal Poly, as an example of a typical agricultural ethics course. This course is recognized as a humanities course that serves as one of the core requirements for liberal arts credit; it is usually team taught. Each instructor has one section with 25 students in a seminar format that meets jointly for lecture–discussions and separately once a week for discussion. Each week students conduct a public forum (town meeting) on selected agricultural issues. Students work as a group to develop specific conflicting roles, which they play during the forum. The debate seeks public consensus rather than winners and losers, and this allows the students to examine other values without having to adopt them as their own.

At Cal Poly the students are evaluated on both written and oral presentations. To provide uniform and consistent evaluation by the instructors in the different sections, each student must satisfy four criteria for his or her ethical decisions (Table 2). These criteria include "sacred" nonutilitarian rights, protection of life and health, protection of rural values and family life, an aesthetics of the environment, an equitable sharing of public support in times of crisis, and a sharing of the risks from the negative and unintended consequences of any technology. We consider future generations in all our

Table 2. Criteria for ethical decisions at Cal Poly State University.

1.	Questions that need to be answered should be established.
2.	Significant side effects should be considered, including economic, social, political, physical, and emotional considerations.
3.	As much technical information as possible should be gathered.
4.	Decisions should be made by reasonably and consistently weighing the risks and benefits of the current policy and all alternatives.

evaluations, and use our Western values while we respect and understand Eastern philosophies (such as Buddhist economies). Finally, we emphasize holistic problem-solving to help students deal with real life situations.

This course is *not* a defense of the agricultural profession against an angry public. Some current practices in agriculture should not be defended. The course trains students — future agricultural professionals — to become articulate and effective in public meetings. All too often current agricultural leaders defeat their purpose by speaking out to defend a narrowly construed objective, rather than listening and learning what others suggest can and should be done. Learning to *listen* to others is a key factor in modern leadership development. We often become uncomfortable when someone challenges us regarding our beliefs and values. We must learn to deal with fear and public apprehension in an effective manner.

Table 3. Case studies for agricultural ethics courses.

A. Used at Cal Poly State University

Agricultural mechanization and displacement of labor
Animal rights–animal welfare
Bovine growth hormone
Efficacy of price support programs
Famine and food aid
Future of the family farm
Green Revolution and its consequences
International debt and food policy
Land use
Loss of genetic diversity
Species rights to a habitat
Sustainability of agricultural production (domestic and international)

B. Other possibilities

Appropriate technology
Distribution of costs and benefits of agricultural research
Endangered species
Energy use in agriculture
Farm worker safety
Food safety
Gender, equality, and credit in agriculture
Genetic engineering
Migrant labor
Overpopulation
Rangeland overgrazing
Regulation of agricultural research

At Cal Poly, agricultural issues are examined in the context of case studies (Table 3A); many other cases could be developed (Table 3B). Readings are collected from a variety of sources concerned with the ethical, technical, scientific, and agricultural aspects of each issue.

The journals *Agriculture and Human Values* and *Journal of Environmental and Agricultural Ethics* publish articles on agricultural ethics. Several recent books are available that focus on agricultural ethics (e.g., Blatz, 1991; Comstock, 1987; Thompson, 1992; Thompson and Stout, 1991; Thompson et al., 1994; Wojcik, 1989). Finally, *Research Ethics, Manuscript Review, and Journal Quality* (Mayland and Sojka, 1992), published by the American Society of Agronomy, focuses on personal ethics and professional roles including conflicts of interest and integrity.

Agricultural Faculty Responsibilities

The greatest barrier facing those teaching agricultural ethics is the battle over turf protection and jargon. While it is crucial to include philosophers and ethicists in the teaching of agricultural ethics, it is important to note that traditionally philosophers and ethicists see their role as teaching ethics, with agriculture as a minor component. Even within philosophy, many philosophers protect their turf by holding in less esteem those who work with applied ethics compared with those who work strictly with traditional ethics. Also, the communication barrier of jargon is as strong in the writings of philosophers as it is in the research presented by any of the scientists in food, agriculture, and natural resources. We need teachers with interdisciplinary competence, who are comfortable with team teaching and possess the ability to argue effectively with other faculty and students. Agricultural faculty who insist on staying within the confines of their narrow disciplines can create problems because they often overemphasize their own expertise. We need to encourage agricultural faculty to broaden their worldviews.

Perspective for Administrators

Administrative support for courses in agricultural ethics is essential. A dean can be helpful in bringing together the agricultural and humanities faculty and in removing some of the institutional barriers that hinder interdisciplinary efforts of this type. The faculty must be chosen carefully. It is best to have agricultural faculty who are highly visible because students see them as role models. I would also offer the following caveat: avoid narrow-minded, single-issue-oriented individuals or people who are on a religious crusade. They are well-intentioned but may do great harm in an agricultural ethics course.

The Benefits of an Agricultural Ethics Course

Students benefit from a course on human values in agriculture in several ways. Such a course develops leadership, sharpens argumentation skills, encourages listening to other views, provides a risk–benefit framework for making sound arguments, enables citizens to become sensitive to value conflicts within our society, encourages decision-making and consensus-building, generates clarity of written and oral expression, and creates an awareness of the limitations of any technology. It is particularly important that we do not try to promote a new technological fix to solve the problems left from the previous technological fix.

What We Need to Learn

A recent survey on curriculum assessment (Love and Yoder, 1989) indicated that 87% of the *faculty* felt values were important, and more than half of them felt values were being attained in the classroom. Also, seven out of every 10 faculty members felt they could teach values. But only one-third of the *graduating seniors* felt they had attained values in their college careers. Obviously, what we do speaks louder than what we teach.

We need to learn to state issues and to express our values in ways that are sensitive to people both inside and outside of agriculture. We need to learn how to ask the right questions. It is important to recognize the role of debate about "fuzzy" and poorly defined issues that have little scientific or factual information. We must not suppress debate about these issues but encourage it. (I believe that much of my training at three land grant institutions emphasized suppressing debate and avoiding conflict.)

We need to learn to make effective decisions on agricultural issues. Nearly all decisions are value laden and lack clear-cut facts. Too often scientists have been taught that science is value free. However, *science is not value free!* The tools that we use in science to measure and assess the world contain values related to some segment of our society. The sooner we can acknowledge this fact, the sooner we will be able to move ahead in understanding ethics.

Conclusion

It is time for a paradigm shift. Richard Bawden suggests that the new paradigm should "accommodate complexity, uncertainty, and even chaos" (Bawden, 1991). The problem one faces is that one cannot begin to accept a new paradigm until one is prepared to let go of the old one. Today we must be able to deal with two views of the world: the world as it exists and the world as it is perceived. Increasingly, we find that these views are different. We must help make these two views more congruent because it is important to foster cooperation, consensus-building, and compromise for the benefit of all people, not just the powerful few.

References

Bawden, R.J. 1991. Systems thinking and practice in agriculture. J. Dairy Sci. 74:2362–2373.

Blatz, C.V. 1991. Ethics and agriculture. An anthology on current issues in world context. Univ. of Idaho Press, Moscow.

Comstock, G. 1987. Is there a moral obligation to save the family farm? Iowa State Univ. Press, Ames.

Love, G.M., and E.P. Yoder. 1989. An assessment of undergraduate education in American colleges of agriculture. Part I: Perceptions of faculty; Part II: Perceptions of graduating seniors; Part III: Perceptions of other university students. College of Agric., Pennsylvania State Univ., University Park.

Mayland, H.F., and R.E. Sojka. 1992. Research ethics, manuscript review, and journal quality. ACS Misc. Publ. ASA, CSSA, and SSSA, Madison, WI.

Merritt, R.H. 1984. Challenges for undergraduate education in agricultural sciences. NACTA J. 28:9–14.

Steinbeck, J. 1951. The log from the Sea of Cortez; the narrative portion of the book, The Sea of Cortez, by John Steinbeck and E.F. Ricketts. Viking Press, New York.

Thompson, P.B. 1992. The ethics of trade and aid: U.S. food policy, foreign competition and the social contract. Cambridge Univ. Press, New York.

Thompson, P.B., and B.A. Stout. 1991. Beyond the large farm: Ethics and research goals for agriculture. Westview Press, Boulder, CO.

Thompson, P.B., R.J. Matthews, and E.O. van Ravenswaay. 1994. Ethics, public policy, and agriculture. Macmillan College Publ. Co., New York.

Wilson, K., and G.E.B. Morren, Jr. 1990. Systems approaches for improvement in agriculture and resource management. Macmillan Publ. Co., New York.

Wojcik, J. 1989. The arguments of agriculture. A casebook in contemporary agricultural controversy. Purdue Univ. Press, West Lafayette, IN.

Glossary

Aesthetics. A branch of philosophy concerned with questions about beauty and art, experiences associated with them, and whether nonarbitrary standards for judgments about beauty and art can be demonstrated. In agricultural ethics, aesthetic questions pertain to the attitudes people take toward the land. The aesthetic attitude contrasts with a practical or instrumental attitude. For example, a person who values land only in terms of its real estate development has a practical, not an aesthetic, attitude toward the land. The aesthetic attitude involves valuing the natural world for itself — for the perceptual details of the surroundings — and the experience of beauty as we perceive it.

Animal rights. The ascription of moral rights to nonhuman animals. The movement for animal rights may be roughly divided into a philosophical branch and a political branch. Political groups, such as People for the Ethical Treatment of Animals or the Animal Liberation Front, take an activist stand, campaigning against the use of animals in testing and research, fur use, food use, and in some cases any use of domestic or wild species. Some of these political groups have resorted to illegal break-ins, property damage, and animal release. The philosophical movement for animal rights has been led by a number of well-known philosophers, including Tom Regan and Bernard Rollin, who have argued from traditional moral rights theory that there are no *morally relevant* differences between human and nonhuman animals that would justify denying rights to animals. These philosophers have presented rational arguments and then have attempted to persuade people to change their attitudes and practices regarding animals. *See* Moral rights.

Animal welfare. The ascription of negative value to the pain and suffering of nonhuman animals. Philosophers (most notably Peter Singer) who argue for the welfare of animals do so from a utilitarian moral framework: since nonhuman animals experience pain, and our moral obligation is to reduce such suffering, then the pain of animals (as well as humans) must be considered in any decision-making process. Under this reasoning process, some animals might be used to benefit humans if greater suffering would result from not using them, but any unnecessary pain to the animals must be mitigated in the process by painless killing, anesthesia and analgesia, adequate housing, and so forth. Critics have charged that utilitarianism could command the sacrifice of some humans to save other humans, or perhaps even of some humans to save animals. *See* Consequentialism and Utilitarianism.

Consequentialism. A moral theory which argues that only the consequences of actions have moral value. Utilitarianism (see definition) is the most important current consequentialist theory. In deciding what to do, the moral agent (see definition) should think about what is likely to happen to the members of the moral community (including the agent, but without giving the self extra weight) in each of the choices open to the agent. One chooses the action that will bring about the best (or least worst) consequences *for the community as a whole.* Implications of consequentialism include: (i) one's own personal life plans and family attachments can have no special value unless these can be justified as contributing to the larger good, and (ii) past actions and intentions have no value and may not be considered unless doing so would contribute to the larger good. It has been charged that these implications (and others) threaten individual liberty, privacy, due process, and other moral protections, and that consequentialist theories require unlimited altruism. *See* Utilitarianism.

Deontological (or deontic) ethics. Moral theories which hold that some acts are morally obligatory whether or not the consequences may be good or bad for some or all of the members of a moral community. Such theories are said to be "duty based," in that their proponents commonly prescribe a set of duties that persons are to perform (e.g., tell the truth, keep promises, and refrain from killing). Immanuel Kant is the best known Western philosopher to set forth a deontic ethics, and his train of thought has been adopted by some moral rights theorists who now propose to derive these duties from the rights of individuals. But deontic ethics can also be justified on utilitarian grounds: one should follow certain rules that prescribe duties because doing so would maximize the overall good for society.

Descriptive. An adjective that applies to statements or propositions about the world and is in contrast to the adjective *prescriptive.* Descriptive statements tell us what *is* the case, whereas prescriptive statements tell us what *ought* to be the case. Descriptive statements come in the form of declarative sentences that can be judged to be true or false, such as "There will be a blue moon this August," or "There are grizzlies in Glacier Park." In arguing from descriptive statements (e.g., "There is elk overpopulation in Yellowstone") alone to reach a prescriptive conclusion (e.g., "The wolf ought to be reintroduced to Yellowstone"), one would be committing a logical fallacy. *Compare* Prescriptive.

Fairness. In morality, a term associated with justice, and given prominence by John Rawls' *A Theory of Justice,* in which he argued for justice as fairness. In Rawls' view, the rules or principles of justice are fair, if (from an ideal position) any rational person who does not know her or his own particular advantages (under conditions Rawls dubbed the "Veil of Ignorance") would choose to live under those rules. Rational persons would choose the rules, knowing that the rules, once chosen, will govern their own lives and will determine the form of government that would be adopted in their society. Rawls assumed that persons are self-interested and want more rather than less liberty, opportunity, wealth, and other goods, and will choose rules that would maximize their opportunity to obtain them while minimizing their risk of losing them should they discover that the "natural lottery" has dealt them a disadvantageous starting place, for example by being born with fewer talents or resources than others. Fairness requires impartiality; each person's interests will be considered equally with those of all of the others, and rules and procedures will be adopted that will guarantee impartiality, at least to the extent practically possible.

Good(s). In classical utilitarian theory, good is happiness, and evil is pain and suffering. John Stuart Mill, in the classical utilitarian tradition, also identifies the good with the satisfaction of desire and evil with the frustration of desire. Some modern utilitarians, such as R.M. Hare (1981), propose simple preferences as indicators of what people actually value with (presumably) their aversions as evils, although Hare qualified this assertion with the proviso that the preference must be something that would be in the individual's interest to have. The proviso serves to rule out self-destructive preferences, for instance. Some utilitarians (Singer, 1979) propose satisfaction of interests as the content of the good, where an interest is something that is truly good for the being. In the rights tradition, Rawls (1971) proposed "primary goods" as those things a rational individual would want, which Rawls enumerated as rights and liberties, powers and opportunities, and income and wealth. Such things are held to be truly in the interest of the individual who acquires them.

Holism. A moral view that directs us to attend to and value a whole system as most important. Holistic medicine, for instance, directs physicians to treat the entire person, rather than simply symptoms or parts. As an agricultural ethic, holism requires decision-making on the basis of the beauty and the intrinsic value of a whole ecosystem, rather than on the basis of concerns about individual plants or animals, or their utility. An inanimate object such as the land is also included as an object within the whole. Implications of this view include the consequence that individuals may be sacrificed for the sake of the whole, and that judgments about beauty and intrinsic value are made invariably from a human perspective. *See* Intrinsic value and Instrumental value.

Instrumental value. A judgment concerning the usefulness, function, or price of an object or experience. An object or experience is instrumentally good if it serves a function or has some use for someone, whereas an object or experience is instrumentally worthless if it has no such function or use, and is therefore *waste*. *Contrast* Intrinsic value.

Intrinsic value. A judgment concerning the good of an object for its own sake, apart from its function or utility. Many writers argue that aesthetic judgments are judgments of intrinsic value and ethical judgments about the dignity of persons are similarly judgments of intrinsic value. For instance, persons are not to be summarily disposed of simply because they are no longer useful or functional. In agricultural ethics, the land has intrinsic value for its own sake, regardless of its usefulness to humans. Judgments of intrinsic value call for actions expressing moral respect. What it is to respect that which has intrinsic value is specified within an ethical system, such as in holism or moral rights theories. *Contrast* Instrumental value.

Justification. The giving of good reasons to support a moral choice or an argument for a moral choice. Justification within a moral theory is given by appeal to moral rules or principles, which are themselves justified by appeal to a more encompassing foundational rule or obligation. Thus, a utilitarian who tells the truth in a particular situation justifies her or his decision by an appeal to a general obligation of truth-telling, which, in turn, is justified by the claim that when people follow the rule of truth-telling, it will promote the general welfare.

Legal rights. Rights that individuals have based on statutes, constitutions, or legal precedent; civil rights are often written in such documents. Legal rights are distinct from and not necessarily correlative to "moral rights."

Moral agent. A being who is mature, rational, and capable of understanding and responding to the commands of morality. Maturity and rationality are required because such beings must be capable of a full understanding of the stake they have in any decision; i.e., they must be aware of how their own self-interest and that of others may be affected or compromised by their decisions. Infants and very young children, the mentally retarded, senile or comatose persons are generally excused from agency and instead are termed as "moral patients" by some thinkers. Similarly, the physical capacity to take action is necessary to agency or the *doing* of some kinds of moral actions. Thus, some physically incapacitated, rational, and mature adults would be excused from some, although not all, moral duties. *Compare* Moral patient.

Moral considerability. Having the requisite characteristics of a member of the moral community; a term used by some to include nonhuman animals, fetuses, future generations, habitats, plants, natural objects, and other beings in the moral sphere.

Moral patient. An individual to whom duties are owed, but who cannot be required to reciprocate in kind. Some individuals may be considered moral patients for all actions, while others are moral patients only for some. Infants and very young children, the severely senile, retarded, or insane are persons whom we are morally required to care for and not to harm or kill, but they themselves are not required to be moral, because they cannot understand the nature of what may be required of them. Persons espousing animal rights and animal welfare include animals in the moral community as moral patients. *Compare* Moral agent.

Moral rights. Rights that individuals have apart from and prior to what is written in law or custom. Rights have been described variously: as protections for the individual against mob rule (Williams, 1973); trumps against the common good (Dworkin, 1977); side-constraints on the efforts of society and those in power to maximize the good for all at the expense of a few (Nozick, 1974); valid claims to the satisfaction of an interest where an interest is something that is truly good for a person, regardless of whether the person knows it or wants it (Feinberg, 1973). Under these descriptions, the reason for adopting moral rights is *not* because having them would maximize the good for all (even though this may occur). Although rights theories have the virtue of protecting individual liberty, when the equal rights of individuals conflict, there seems to be no guidance for deciding what to do. This defect in the theory leads to a rejoinder by utilitarians that rights are ultimately justifiable only in a utilitarian framework, even though the core idea of having a right overrides utilitarian concerns. *See* Legal rights.

Norm (normative). A principle of right action or aesthetic judgment. Relating to, or prescribing norms or standards of judgment or conduct.

Normative conceptualization. Conceiving of or thinking about norms and values that are evaluative or prescriptive. *See* Prescriptive.

Prescriptive. In contrast to *descriptive*, this adjective is applied to statements or propositions about morality or values or both. Prescriptive statements tell us what we *ought* to do or what *ought* to be the case, whereas descriptive statements tell us what *is* the case. Prescriptive statements may also come in the form of commands, such as "Do not kill!" Commands cannot be true or false, but are uttered to direct us to act. Attempting to deduce a command or a prescriptive claim from facts alone is a logical fallacy. *See* Descriptive.

Teleological. Having goals, aims, purposes, or intentions. A teleological moral theory is one in which actions are taken to achieve a specified end. Consequentialist (and utilitarian) moral theories are teleological because the good (e.g., happiness, satisfaction of desires, preferences) is specified and intended for realization in an individual action or policy statement. Rights theories are nonteleological insofar as they specify that right actions are independent of the good; that is, right actions are accomplished by following moral rules, rather than maximizing the good.

These rules are arrived at through a nonteleological process, for example, a social contract.

Utilitarianism. A moral theory directing agents to act so as to maximize the good (or minimize suffering, if positive good cannot be attained) for all who will be affected by the decision-maker's choice. The method for determining the good is to consider each member of the moral community as counting for "one and no more than one," calculate the good or evil that will befall each member, and sum these values for each possible choice. The good of the community is the sum of the interests of the individuals. Whatever is actually valued, though, the moral agent is to consider only the consequences of her or his actions. Intentions and commitments of the past have value only insofar as they contribute to future good consequences. *Compare* Consequentialism.

References

Dworkin, R. 1977. Taking rights seriously. Harvard Univ. Press, Cambridge, MA.

Feinberg, J. 1973. Social philosophy. Prentice-Hall, Englewood Cliffs, NJ.

Hare, R.M. 1981. Moral thinking: Its levels, method, and point. Clarendon Press, New York.

Nozick, R. 1974. Anarchy, state, and utopia. Basic Books, New York.

Rawls, J. 1971. A theory of justice. Belknap Press of Harvard Univ., Cambridge, MA.

Singer, P. 1979. Practical ethics. Cambridge Univ. Press, New York.

Williams, B. 1973. A critique of utilitarianism. p. 77–150. *In* J.J.C. Smart and B. Williams (ed.) Utilitarianism; for and against. Cambridge Univ. Press, Cambridge, England.

Biographical Sketches

Charles V. Blatz is Associate Professor and Head of the Department of Philosophy at the University of Toledo (Ohio). He is a founding member of the International Development Ethics Association and the editor of *Ethics and Agriculture: An Anthology on Current Issues in World Context* (1991).

Gary Comstock is Associate Professor in the Department of Philosophy at Iowa State University (Ames). He is the coordinator of the Bioethics Program at Iowa State and the editor of *Is There a Moral Obligation to Save the Family Farm?* (1987).

Stanley E. Curtis is Professor and Head of the Department of Dairy and Animal Science at The Pennsylvania State University (University Park). He is the current president of the American Society of Animal Science and the editor of *Guide to the Care and Use of Agricultural Animals in Agricultural Research and Teaching* (1988).

Frederick Ferré is Research Professor in the Department of Philosophy at the University of Georgia (Athens). He is the author of many books, the most recent of which is *Hellfire and Lightning Rods: Liberating Science, Technology, and Religion* (1993). He is also the general editor of the journal *Research in Philosophy and Technology*.

C. Dean Freudenberger is Professor of Church and Society at Luther Northwestern Theological Seminary (St. Paul, MN). A strong proponent of regenerative agriculture, Dr. Freudenberger is the author of *Global Dust Bowl: Can We Stop the Destruction of the Land Before It's Too Late?* (1990), *Food for Tomorrow?* (1984), and *Christian Responsibility in a Hungry World* (1976).

Peter G. Hartel is Associate Professor in the Department of Crop and Soil Sciences at the University of Georgia (Athens). A soil microbiologist by training, Dr. Hartel is the program coordinator of the Environmental Ethics Certificate Program at the University of Georgia. He has taught agricultural ethics since 1988.

Thomas A Ruehr is Professor in the Soil Science Department at California Polytechnic State University (San Luis Obispo). Along with philosopher Stan Dundon, he pioneered the first university course in agricultural ethics in 1984. He has served as co-chair of the USDA's Curriculum Development Program for agricultural ethics and public policy.

311458